DEMOCRACY SPEAKS MANY TONGUES

DEMOCRACY SPEAKS
MANY TONGUES

Community Development Around the World

RICHARD WAVERLY POSTON

HARPER & ROW, PUBLISHERS, NEW YORK AND EVANSTON

12 1 68   *coucecrip Beath*   4.25

To

Marjorie, Gregory, and Stephanie

CONTENTS

FOREWORD

This book is about community development and much more. It raises issues far beyond its overt purpose: to explore a variety of such programs around the world. Indirectly, and yet quite pointedly, Richard Poston calls our attention to the critical universal problem of our time: man's search for his identity and purpose.

The intellectual search for understanding takes many forms. We have taken intensive looks at man's psychological development, and we have learned much about his patterns of coping with problems. We know something of the relevance of productive work and the ability of man to deal meaningfully with his environment and fellow man. Other searchers have attempted to understand the institutions created by man: his work groups, his schools, his communities, and his governments. In these and many other areas of study one problem stands out clearly: The critical question for the emerging world, both the underdeveloped nations and ourselves, is the need to find ways for human beings not to be overwhelmed by the technical achievements or needs of people and nations. We must find ways of coping with the complexity of our society; with the incomprehensible nature of conflicting values, goals, beliefs, motivations, or methods of solution.

Man has attempted to solve these problems by better machinery, better computers, and larger budgets for aid or arms, as well as by a list of other materialistic technical tools. Much has been "successful" and yet the problems remain, become more acute, more frightening. Delinquency of juvenile or adult white collar variety becomes more common; aggressiveness, revolutions, rebellions, withdrawals from participation, are some of the ways people of the world have tried to deal with these problems and are overwhelmed. A turning inward and searching for the self through religion and psychology or psychiatry, a willingness to enlist for menial service programs or for the Peace Corps are further, perhaps more positive, reflections of man's solutions. The whole world is in turmoil, ourselves included; social and antisocial solutions are being attempted more or less successfully.

Quiet, and heretofore unsung, are the attempts of the community developers to bring meaning to man by helping him to help himself and to use the magnificent tools now potentially available to all. Poston celebrates these heroes, though most of them do their work with no sense of glory or history, they are only heroes to the people with whom they work.

Poston was once called a "psychiatrist for sick communities," and indeed he is. Whereas a psychiatrist deals with but one minuscule part of the world, a single patient, Poston typifies the best of the broader approach. Like the psychiatrist, but with no other theoretical connection, he waits to be asked for help; he tries to understand the total problem; he gently guides his "patient" to find new ways to solve old problems and to find new resources within and outside itself. Resolutions and answers cannot be determined by the community developer; he only has the skill to help individuals, groups, and communities find their own answers through self help. As they find these answers they find themselves, and they find new meaning through their work and living.

Against a background of the technical world, against the arms race and the vast economic support now available, these small attempts that Poston reports may seem impossibly insignificant. Yet they may hold the secret to meaning for our life today.

Though Poston writes of others in this book, he could very well have written of himself. He is a special and unique person. You but meet him, and he has an impact that is challenging and vital. He is always on the move, always searching for new ideas, helping people, and teaching community development to all who will listen. What is most striking is not his ability to analyze what community development is and means—which he does well—but the way he works, the way he reports what he sees. What he has seen in his voyage of discovery should have great meaning to us all, at home and abroad. His report may make many persons uncomfortable. When inappropriate and inadequate solutions to complicated and confused situations are pointed out, the process is often disturbing.

I commend this work with its message to those who should and must read this book: all of us.

Leonard J. Duhl, M.D.

National Institutes of Health
Washington, D. C.
April 1962

INTRODUCTION

Probably no operation of the United States government has been more widely criticized, both at home and abroad, than foreign aid operations in the newly developing areas of the world. Overseas, America has been accused of doing too little too late, of being highhanded, and of being unable to understand the culture and problems of the countries being aided. Critics at home have said that foreign aid is a handout, a waste, an effort that is unappreciated and unnecessary. Others have said that if we would engage in foreign aid solely for humanitarian purposes and without self-interest, more would be accomplished and America would be more widely appreciated. It is true that many of the countries receiving huge amounts of United States aid have become some of America's sharpest critics. Many have frequently taken sides with the Soviet Union, and some have joined with the Soviets completely.

All of these criticisms contain elements of truth, except the one that says foreign aid is unnecessary. The tensions and the human miseries of today's world have made foreign aid one of the most important operations of the United States, and inasmuch as the world situation has grown steadily worse ever since the program began, foreign aid is more needed now than ever. Indeed, it is doubtful that any living American will see the day when foreign aid is no longer needed.

All countries know that no nation takes any action without regard for its own national interests. The Constitution of the United States prohibits the expenditure of the people's money unless it is expressly in the national interest. Yet the fact is that America has been more generous than any other nation in world history in its efforts to aid other countries. Foreign aid is motivated by humanitarian principles. It must help the downtrodden, the distressed, the suffering. But if these purposes are to be accomplished, foreign aid must at the same time become a practical instrument of international politics to help build and strengthen the foundations of freedom, and in that way serve the national interests of the United States as well as the interests of others. The question is not whether foreign aid is needed, but the type of programs through which it is extended and the way those programs are carried out.

This is a book about a little-noticed program called community development which can make it possible for foreign aid to build freedom in today's world, to serve thereby the interests of others and of America, and do it effectively.

As a research professor at Southern Illinois University traveling as a consultant to CARE, the Cooperative for American Relief Everywhere, and with a grant from the Rockefeller Foundation, I have made a series of studies of American foreign aid operations during the past two years in many of the countries of Latin America, Southern Europe, the Middle East, South and Southeast Asia, and the Far East. I have seen the rising tide of expectations, the grinding poverty, the hunger, the bleakness, and the countless obstacles to progress that exist in these areas. In a way that I could not have conceived without seeing for myself, I have learned of the terror and the threat to freedom and to all standards of human decency which these conditions pose.

In these newly developing areas I found another world of which America until recently was hardly aware— a world in which the great masses of the people have lived for centuries in a state of social and political stupor, ruled over by foreigners, by local demagogues, or by a small elite that profited and grew rich without concern for the masses. Docile, inert, illiterate, politically mute, resigned to their fate, and with no trace of self-reliance or even of a sense of their rights as human beings, these vast millions existed as an almost sub-human element of the earth's population without stirring or complaining, while the advanced democracies of the West developed and leveled off in complacency almost unconscious of the existence of this other world.

But suddenly this other world was ignited by a surge of nationalism, a drive for independence, and for progress into the family of nations. Suddenly the millions who had accepted their fate were no longer willing to continue their acceptance. Suddenly they began to cry out for political equality, for liberty, for education, for food, for their share of the earth's plenty. They began to rise up, to launch out, and as this stirring gained momentum, a new and violent revolutionary force began to sweep over the earth. But the ancient conditions of backwardness, poverty, and oppression have been too long and too firmly established to yield either easily or quickly. And so the battle was joined between the forces of yesterday and the forces of tomorrow. Meanwhile, the agents of communism, quick to sense the advantage which this battle presented for the Communist purpose of world domination, moved in increasing numbers to exploit that advantage cunningly and vigorously.

Because of America's historic ideals of freedom and concern for humanitarian principles, and because United States leaders recognized what was at stake in the struggle that had begun, America entered into a worldwide program of foreign aid, but with far less aggressiveness and imagination than was needed. While the agents of communism pressed their deadly game, America went about its business, debated whether foreign aid was necessary, permitted bureaucrats in the various sections of its foreign aid organization to argue and bicker among themselves over professional prestige and program control, indulged in the wishful thought that being a generous world spender ought to take care of the newly developing countries, and held academic discussions on whether people in other lands should be disturbed from their traditional patterns of life and whether they were capable of assuming the responsibilities of democracy.

In America there was a general assumption that the newly developing countries should stabilize their governments and be friendly toward us because we were helping them to build roads, dams, and other physical amenities, and we were sending out technicians in agricultural extension and other standard American occupations to show the primitive people new techniques and skills.

But when I began traveling around the world, I was overwhelmed by the appalling failure of more than ten years of American foreign aid. It was almost unbelievable to see how little had been accomplished, considering the billions that had been spent, and to realize how little had filtered down to the people where it was needed. American foreign aid was not accomplishing its purpose of building economies in which the great masses of the people could gain notable personal benefit or satisfy their desires for material progress. It was failing to create an effective organized effort for democracy, and it was making no headway toward satisfying the idealism of a world social revolution. After more than a decade it had created neither a sufficient sense of social and political responsibility nor the social and administrative machinery necessary to satisfy man's material needs and remove the conditions that were favorable to communism.

Now, with a new Agency for International Development, and with American youth being sent to all parts of the world as Peace Corps volunteers, the United States confronts a global atmosphere of turmoil, tension, and struggle. This is not merely a struggle between Western power and Communist power. It is a struggle between the ideals of liberty and the dogma of tyranny. It is a struggle in which the vast populations of the newly developing countries of the world will play a decisive role, but in which the direction to be chosen by these populations will depend largely upon the actions of America and her allies, and the Soviet Union and her allies. This is the great contest that is being waged in the world today, and it is now time for the American people to recognize that we are engaged in that contest whether we like it or not; for if freedom is to survive, if World War III is to be avoided, America must apply herself more vigorously than she has in the past to the practical job of winning that contest.

No one who has witnessed the conditions of the underdeveloped world, which will be described in this account, can properly argue against the necessity of continued American foreign aid. But unless that aid is delivered in such a way as to reduce the social and political unrest and strengthen and multiply the forces of freedom in the newly developing countries, America will unwittingly permit the ultimate triumph of communism and the consequent loss of the basic ideals of human dignity for which the American people have been willing to support foreign aid expenditures.

Certainly, it is true that not all peoples are yet ready for the responsibilities of democracy. But this is no reason to retreat from the task of helping to build the organizational basis for these responsibilities. Certainly, it would be inappropriate for America to try to make over other countries in her own image. But this should not prevent us from exercising leadership that will help hasten the development of self-determination, and release the latent capacities for the exercise of social and political responsibility.

America herself is symbolic of the revolutionary spirit of freedom that the newly developing countries are seeking, and unless American officials and technicians supply effective leadership for the encouragement of that spirit at the level of actual operations where foreign aid counts, more and more countries will turn to the fleeting hope of communism or to some other form of regimentation.

Democracy is actually the only thing that America has to offer the world that is any different from communism. But unless a diligent effort is made to help build and strengthen the machinery through which democracy can be effectively applied to man's social and economic advance, unless such an effort is pursued by a missionary zeal at least equal to the zeal by which the Communists work for their methods, there is no hope for democracy in the world struggle of today, regardless of how many billions may be appropriated for American foreign aid. This is the background against which this book is written.

Essentially, this is a story of the struggle for freedom and economic decency which is being waged against tremendous odds by bold people in newly developing countries around the world. It is not fiction. The people, the places, and the events are real. In this story many Americans have played heroic parts, but in many respects the United States foreign aid agency has in itself been one of the obstacles.

The story which is told in this account is not a finished one; it is still being written in actions and events that are now in process—actions and events that at this moment are determining not only the destiny of the underdeveloped world, but of the human race, including every American. The specific events that I will relate, the actions of the men and women which have been a part of these events, are now history. But the principles and the lessons to be drawn from them are applicable today, tomorrow, and in the years ahead.

Richard Waverly Poston

Carbondale, Illinois
March 1962

1

A WOMAN OF VISION AND COURAGE

DEEP IN THE COFFEE AND BANANA COUNTRY OF TROPICAL Central America, in the Republic of Guatemala, lives a tall, dark-haired woman of aristocratic Spanish descent whose personal attack on the ancient forces of poverty has become a demonstration of the kind of leadership that must be found and supported if democracy is to succeed in the under-developed world. Her name is Señora Elisa Molina de Stahl —"Moli" for short.

From her father, who was one of the wealthiest planters in the mountainous country surrounding the old Spanish city of Quezaltenango, she absorbed a "social emotion" for the conditions of life that prevail among three-fourths of the people of Guatemala. This woman has the vision to see the human squalor that infests her beautiful country—a squalor that is no more than a hazy image in the collective conscious-ness of the Latin elite.

In this part of the world, rich coffee plantations—*fincas*—stretch over vast reaches of rugged terrain. Wealthy land-owners are justly proud of their coffee trees, their fine hunt-ing dogs, sleek cattle, and horses of pure-bred stock. It is a land of fiestas, marimba bands, fine liqueurs, of beautiful señoritas for gentlemen well-bred in the old Latin tradition —in short, a life of high Spanish society to be enjoyed and

1

preserved. Certainly, it is not a life to spoil by a concern for the majority of the people who do not share in its benefits.

Most of the people are Indians descended from the Mayan civilization long ago subjugated by the Spanish *conquistadors,* or they are *mestizos,* a mixed race derived from pleasures provided the early Spanish conquerors by Indian women. These people are simply an adjunct to Spanish society, and it is the landowning class, comprising the upper 2 per cent, who provide them with the meager support they receive. All this has long been an established part of life and habit in this part of the world.

But because of the strange social emotion that has become a part of the personal equipment of Moli Stahl, her vision has caused her to form a different image of life in the coffee country. In this land of great estates with their rolling grounds, thick grass, and climbing vines of bright purple bougainvillaea, Moli has learned to see other elements—ugly, depraved, human elements—that disturb the natural serenity.

She has learned to see the great manor houses that crown the hills and their feudal lords, owners of a nation. In the lower lands of the *fincas* she sees the clusters of grass, bamboo, and crude wooden one-room huts of the peon families who from early morning until late evening perform the human labor that makes the *fincas* productive.

Inside these one-room huts are the rough boards and woven palm mats that serve as beds, a rough table and chairs, the bony dogs of the peon family, and the blackened, filth-littered, bare earthen floor. From an open stone hearth in one corner of the room that provides a place to cook what little food there might be, a haze of smoke rises upward to escape partly through cracks in the walls, and gradually seep out through the grass-thatched roof.

Crowded together in these dark, smoke-filled huts are the families of brown-skinned people, sometimes a dozen or more to a hut, fathers and mothers, sons, daughters, in-laws, children naked from the waist down, and the few who have somehow managed to survive to old age. In these tiny huts with no facilities for the discharge of human waste except the ground, the people live, sleep, eat, give birth to their babies, care for their personal needs, fall victim to intestinal parasites, malaria, and other tropical disease, and either manage without doctors or die. The loss of women from childbirth is high. Many, perhaps the fortunate, fail to live past infancy. Many die from sheer physical weakness and malnutrition.

In the larger *fincas* there are several such clusters of peon homes, often making a population of more than a thousand. Usually there is a Roman Catholic Church, and in some *fincas,* a school poorly attended, because from six or seven years of age, the children's labor is needed to help earn the family's food. Rarely does the family have what might be called a balanced diet. There is little time for leisure and virtually no recreation, except for the biological pleasures experienced in the crowded huts, and the fleeting thrills that come from the brief meetings of young people at the community spring where the girls go each day to fill the family earthen water jug, and where older women gather to do the family washing. Each *finca* is a self-contained community.

To the workers, the owner is boss, father, *patrón,* almost God. In a legal sense the workers are not slaves. They are free to leave if they wish. But few ever leave, for to them the *finca* is home and there is no other place to go. Indeed, most of them live in daily fear that if they should displease the *patrón* they might be forced to leave, and what then would they do?

In the tenant sharecropper lands and the mountain villages and small towns outside the *fincas,* life is no better but in many respects worse. No, these people are not slaves. They are the illiterate inert mass of theoretically free men who make up the bulk of human society in Guatemala, captives of a rigid social and economic system that has existed for longer than the oldest can remember, in which work, starvation, disease, subservience, fatalism, and death have for centuries been the basic elements of life.

These are some of the elements that loom in the image of

her country as seen by Señora Elisa Molina de Stahl, and it is the necessity for this image to be changed that has become the driving force of her life. But there are other elements— among them the chaotic elements of turmoil and political in- stability—that have plagued her country since she was a little girl. In 1931, while she was just thirteen, Gorge Ubico became the president of Guatemala and established an ex- treme right-wing dictatorship. As the tyranny of the dictator grew, her country became hopelessly lost in a maze of po- litical edicts, moral corruption, and starvation. All sem- blance of the public interest was ignored, and an armed band of secret police enforced the iron rule of the regime.

Finally, in 1944, the people could no longer be contained. A mob marched on the national palace shouting for the dictator's resignation. A state of siege was declared. Stores, shops, and offices closed. Business came to a halt. In July of that year Ubico resigned in favor of a committee of three generals, led by Federico Ponce, a political opportunist who took control of the government and emerged as the new president of the republic. Under Ponce, the country was soon bathed in corruption even worse than before. The press was placed under censorship; Alejandro Cordova, editor of the newspaper *El Imparcial,* who dared to defy the new regime, was murdered. Confusion again spread through the capital. A group of disgruntled army officers seized the gov- ernment arsenal. Ponce fled and another temporary govern- ment came to power. Dr. Juan José Arévalo, a wily, brilliant, and Machiavellian individual, became the presi- dential candidate of the revolution, and in an overwhelming victory was elected president of the republic for a six-year term. That was March 1945. From that time on the agents of communism gained an increasingly tighter hold on the reins of government.

In 1938, Moli, one of Guatemala's most attractive young women, married a prominent young businessman, Rodolfo Stahl, "Fito," as she called him, and later became the mother of two boys, Rodolfo and Roberto. Moli and Fito knew, as did many others, that if Guatemala were to survive as anything resembling a free society the dictator had to go. But as the pendulum began to swing, they realized that in the intoxicating moments of release from Ubico's despotism, their country was being drawn into the equally horrible morass of communism.

From her earliest childhood Moli had learned that if any lasting improvement were to be made in the social and economic fabric of her country, it would have to come through the advancement of freedom and civic determination from the bottom up, coupled with aggressive and dedicated leadership from the top. Through the latter half of the forties while her children were very young, she studied ways to solve this overwhelming problem. Her ideas were not quickly crystallized, but she soon realized that to bring about the social transformation that Guatemala needed, a truly democratic leadership would have to be projected into every community in her country, working directly with the people to build an organized mass effort from below. Leaders would have to be employed from the national level to help the people attain modern sanitation and better health, better homes, better economic standards, and above all teach them how to think, organize, plan, and take action to do these things for themselves, so that viable democratic institutions and initiative could be built into the society at the local level.

Moli also reasoned that to make such a national program possible, a whole new pattern of attitudes had to be implanted in Guatemala—attitudes such as the development of individual responsibility among the masses for the welfare of their own society. Attitudes would have to be cultivated that would cause people throughout the country, both peasants and elite, to want to support and help carry out voluntary programs in which all citizens from the highest to the lowest would begin to realize their interdependence, and come to know and appreciate the needs of the less fortunate. As Moli saw it, a national conscience would have to be molded that would make people want to engage in a wide range of citizen action projects from which the people could not only improve their material status, but learn the meanings of democratic action. In her mind this was the real inner need of Guatemala.

Her dream was ambitious and vague; it seemed too far beyond the current level of public comprehension to be realized. To initiate the kind of effort she had envisaged, she felt that she first needed a definite project that could be easily explained to the people—a tool, an instrument, in the form of a nationwide program to deal with a specific social problem. Such a project, she reasoned, would give her something to dramatize the attitudes of social responsibility that would then allow her to proceed step by step with the unfolding of her idea for the building of a nationwide civic effort. In 1949, with two years of the Arévalo regime yet to go, she found her opportunity.

In Guatemala City a committee for the blind had been started and Moli was asked to become its chairman. The committee, which included the wife of the minister of defense, Jacobo Arbenz, had set up a small school for blind people, but it was not a strong organization and in effect had no program. The school was in pitiful condition. It had no trained personnel, no equipment, and no money. But it was the only institution for the care of the blind in Guatemala.

For many years the streets of Guatemala City had been filled with blind beggars reaching out for alms. Many of them had no place but the streets in which to live, and the public seemed indifferent even to their identity. Some of the streets downtown became so filled with these human castoffs that passers-by sometimes found it difficult to avoid stepping on them. People would drop coins into their outstretched hands and let it go at that.

There were many people in Guatemala City, as there are in all cities, with good intentions. But the idea of helping beggars who cluttered the streets to develop into self-sustaining, productive members of society was given no more attention than the thought of helping to develop initiative and self-reliance in the mass of Indian and *mestizo* peasants who made up the bulk of the country's population. Never in the country's history had there been a sufficient public conscience to make possible even a general fund-raising campaign for a program of social service. It would have been unthinkable for anyone to walk into a business establishment or knock on doors up and down a city residential street for such a purpose. It was not that people were opposed to organized charities; it was just that such things were not done. True, a few people had in the past tried to raise a little money for one cause or another, but without affecting the national complacency. Charity was limited to alms-giving or to the special donations of the wealthy.

Against this established tradition, Moli knew it would not be simple to produce the support she would need for a modern program to help prevent blindness and to rehabilitate the afflicted. Her first task was to reverse a long history of established attitudes toward charity. She had to cultivate a public understanding of modern social service. If she could accomplish this change, she would then be in a position to accomplish many others. This was to be her entering wedge for the cultivation of a public conscience. Each step would lead to the next. With this reasoning in mind, she began working on her first step.

Soon, she devoted herself full time, without pay, to the cause, serving both as chairman of the committee for the blind and as its operating executive director. Under her leadership, the committee laid plans for an institution designed to provide the blind with a suitable place to live and work, and to enter into an organized program of treatment, education, and rehabilitation. But no plans could be put into effect without money, and it was in this matter of financing that she saw her greatest opportunity to cultivate support from large numbers of people.

She arranged a special meeting with the Guatemala City newspaper association, the APG. Virtually every newspaperman in the city responded to her appeal and by the time she had finished outlining her proposition, the working press had agreed unanimously to support a campaign of public education and fund raising.

"We must think not merely of an asylum for the blind,"

she told them, "or of just a way to get beggars off the streets. We must plan for the total needs of blind people as human beings."

In her own personable way, Moli explained that what was needed was a modern service institution staffed by doctors, nurses, teachers, vocational training specialists, social workers, and others especially trained to work with the blind. They would need special equipment, a continuous supply of good food, and a modern, sanitary kitchen.

"Our purpose," she said, "will be to help these people overcome their handicap of blindness and whatever other physical or emotional problems they may have. We want to make it possible for them to develop into self-respecting, responsible, productive citizens, able and willing to care for themselves and contribute to the progress of our country."

To most people in Guatemala this was a whole new line of thought, but with Moli to put it across it made sense to the newsmen.

"To do this," she told them, "we must not let the work of the committee for the blind become the responsibility of just a few people. We must get thousands of people to contribute something, no matter how little, so that the time will come when people throughout all Guatemala will think of this as their program and their responsibility."

She proposed an appeal that would encourage people to contribute their services as well as their money. The committee, she explained, would not be able to pay for all the specialists and other workers that would be needed, and there would be many opportunities for volunteer work from all kinds of people.

She was now ready for the big question she knew was in all their minds. How much money would it take to get started? For this purpose she proposed that a special week be set aside to be known as the "Week for the Blind."

"And in that one week," she announced, "we will raise $20,000."

The newsmen were visibly startled. It was fantastic. No such thing had ever been done. They all had high regard for

Moli, but now they thought she was talking like a dreamer. They assured her they were all for her ideas, but two thousand dollars would be more realistic.

Moli looked squarely at them and started over. "We've got to raise $20,000; we can, and we will!"

The newsmen congratulated her as the meeting ended. They were sold on her ideas and her enthusiasm, but still skeptical about the amount that could be raised. Indeed, nobody but Moli thought they could come even close to her goal. But under her personal direction, the Week for the Blind was proclaimed, the campaign began, and everybody she approached went to work.

Never in the history of Guatemala had there been such publicity for a social problem. Every newspaper in the city carried banner headlines for the special week and devoted pages of copy to the new concept of social responsibility. To turn public attention on the Week for the Blind and build the new public attitudes she felt were essential to her country's future, Moli went all over town day and night, speaking to groups, soliciting individuals, and mobilizing every medium of public communication, radio stations, theatres, church leaders, student groups, and business and professional organizations.

At the week's end her campaign goal had not only been reached, but well over-subscribed. In this city which never in its history had witnessed a public fund-raising drive for anything, thousands of people had raised in one week more than $25,000 for the committee for the blind, and because of Moli's organizational ability, the total campaign cost to the committee was virtually nothing.

A major victory had been won not only for the blind, but for the whole future of social service in Guatemala. An important break had been made with the past. New confidence had been established, and Moli and her faithful newsmen had formed a personal alliance for greater struggles yet to come.

Moli next moved to seek technical assistance from the United Nations for program planning, only to be told that the UN could not supply such assistance without a formal request from the government of Guatemala. She promptly arranged for the official request, and then contacted the American Foundation for Overseas Blind. Within a short time she fortified herself with the best technical advisors she could get, and the committee began working out the fine points of the modern program she insisted they must have. One of the most difficult obstacles was that in Guatemala there were no trained people available for the kind of staff needed to operate such a program. So Moli began raising funds for scholarships with which to get a staff trained, while at the same time recruiting volunteers to put into effect the plans that were now being worked out with the aid of her technical advisors from overseas.

Meanwhile, an outright pro-Communist, Colonel Jacobo Arbenz, whose wife was a member of the committee for the blind, became the president of Guatemala and within a short time the Communists gained complete control of the government. Recognizing the effectiveness of Moli Stahl's operation, the leftist leaders decided to recruit her for their political cause and take over the program she had started, which by this time had become one of the most popular and best-known institutions in the capital city. Moli promptly made it known that she would have no part in the Communist conspiracy and that if the government gained control of the program, which now included a modern school for the blind, it would no longer have any value as a public service. But the government was determined.

For months pressure was built up against her by government officials and party functionaries, even by a group of the blind people themselves whom the Communist agents had successfully agitated into rebellion against Moli's leadership. By these tactics it was expected that she would step aside and accede to the government's wishes. But Moli would not step aside.

The situation was becoming embarrassing to the government. Speeches calling for action were being voiced in the Communist-dominated congress. Determined to get her out of the way, one of the top ministers of the Arbenz cabinet went to Moli's office and told her the time had come when it was necessary for her to turn the school for the blind over to the government.

Her response was direct.

"I cannot do this for two very good reasons. The government would not operate our program as well as we are doing it, and my first concern is for the people we serve. Secondly, this institution does not belong to me personally, and both on legal and moral grounds I have no right to turn it over to anybody."

The minister tried to interrupt, but she cut him off.

"This institution belongs to the citizens who have contributed to it. If it is the consensus of all these people that it should be delivered to the government, then I have no alternative. But until I am convinced that this is the case, I will not hand it over to you. I will keep faith with the people I represent and carry out their wishes, not yours."

"The government can do this work better than any private organization," said the minister, "just as we run the General Hospital."

"The hospital is a good example," she replied. "It does not even have cotton and proper sanitation for the patients. My answer to you is no."

There was no dealing with this woman. The minister left. That night an unknown person kept ringing Moli's telephone threatening personal violence to her and members of her family. Two days later she received an unsigned note in the mail which read, "You have two children we know you love. You had better choose between your children and your attitude toward the school for the blind."

The morning after the visit from the minister she went to her newspaper friends, told them what was happening, and asked whether or not they would continue to support her. With but one exception the response to stay with her was unanimous. That exception, the government's semi-official newspaper *Tribuna Popular,* attacked her viciously, publishing false statements about her personal integrity and her competence.

To Moli, the more they threatened, the greater became

the challenge to her ideals. And she was not without support. All but one member of the committee for the blind, Señora Arbenz, conspicuous by her absence, stood with her. Business and professional people throughout the city applauded her courage, and her family stayed solidly behind her. Her personal alliance with the working press never dimmed, as a barrage of supporting copy poured forth to counteract the lies being published by *Tribuna Popular*. Even the Communists had to reckon with one undeniable truth—Elisa Molina de Stahl had grown into a popular public leader in Guatemala and had now become something of a test for the Arbenz government.

One day in her downtown office she received a telephone call from the minister of health ordering her to go with him to the school for the blind, because "today the government is officially taking control of the school."

Moli stalled for time, and the minister agreed to grant a few minutes' delay. During those few minutes she organized a telephone alert to all members of the committee for the blind and called her attorney and her newspaper friends. Then she drove to the minister's office to accompany him to the official government possession ceremony.

Upon arrival at the school she was confronted by a large crowd which had been assembled by Communist agents. In it there were even blind students from the school itself. The crowd had been skillfully worked into a surly, milling mob armed with clubs and stones. As Moli and the minister drove up, the mob pressed close to her car, yelling and threatening.

Four of her newspaper friends pushed their way between her and the mob. One of them, courageously risking his own safety, said in a loud voice so the minister could hear, "Don't worry. Everything will work out. We are with you."

Moli faced the minister and said, "If anything happens to me you will be personally responsible."

The minister ordered the crowd to stand aside. He and Moli and the four newspapermen pushed their way into the building. Inside, government officials and members of the official party had gathered for the kill. Much to the surprise

of the minister, there too were all members of the committee for the blind, except Señora Arbenz, and several important political leaders, including the ex-president of the
congress under Arévalo, who had pledged their support to
Moli despite the official policy.

Addressing the group, the minister told them this was a
routine matter which had nothing to do with politics and he
did not understand the presence of those people who were
sitting with the committee. He explained that it was the
decision of the government that the school for the blind
could best be handled by the government, and therefore he
was assuming control. He explained further that he would
read an official proclamation which would serve as public
notice of the action, and that Señora Stahl, in her capacity
as chairman of the committee for the blind, would sign in
acknowledgment.

Moli's attorney whispered that she had no alternative but
to sign.

But before the minister began reading, she made a statement of her own for public notice. "All right, here is the
school. Under my protest you are taking over. But I want it
stated on the record that I am signing this paper only under
protest, and that we will fight this to the end. This is only
the beginning. Maybe you think you are ahead for now, but
we will see who wins in the end. You have the force and the
power. You can do anything you want. But we have a greater
force, not material, but very strong. Our force is spiritual.
And our force will win."

The minister read the proclamation. Moli signed.

"Now," she said, "you have opened fire. The battle is on."

For nearly six months she remained at her post refusing
to move out, with the government threatening physical
action against her, but reluctant to follow through.

Then something happened that changed the whole situation. From deep in the mountains of Honduras to the south
an army under the leadership of a young exile, Castillo
Armas, began to move. Suddenly, Guatemala City became
chaos. War planes buzzed the city dropping leaflets appeal-

ing to the people to rebel, that liberation was near. The Communists became panicky. In early morning hours trucks loaded with dead bodies, victims of the Arbenz government's last efforts to control the population, rolled through the streets. For three days the city was under bombardment. Moli's school for the blind was forgotten by the leftist agents. Arbenz fled, and on July 3, 1954, Castillo Armas with his rebel forces marched triumphantly into the city, welcomed by thousands of cheering spectators who lined the streets of his approach. Communism had been defeated, at least for the time being, in Guatemala.

Next day on the Fourth of July at a United States Embassy party, Señora Stahl and Castillo Armas, who a few months later became the president of Guatemala, met in person. With the help of the new president, Moli greatly expanded the operations of the committee for the blind until within a few years Guatemala had on a nationwide scale one of the most modern and complete programs in all Latin America for the prevention of both blindness and deafness, and for the rehabilitation of persons afflicted with either of these handicaps, including fully-equipped diagnostic and treatment centers, schools, a housing project, and a manufacturing plant for the employment of blind and deaf workers. The once familiar scene of blind beggars in the streets with no place to go and no one to care had virtually disappeared from Guatemala City. With the committee firmly established and a well-trained staff at work, she now had completed the first step in her plan for the building of a new public attitude of social responsibility, and the development of social progress in the life of her country.

Moli was now ready to enlarge her efforts into a program in which whole communities would become organized for self-improvement. In her projection of this idea she worked on the belief that Guatemala's greatest problem was its rural areas in which most of the people lived, and that in these areas it was the communities themselves that were sick and, therefore, needed to be changed. How could people who lived all their lives in communities that were sick and unwholesome be expected to develop into responsible citizens? On the basis of this reasoning, she envisaged a program of community development—the over-all improvement of community life by the people themselves.

Not even the reforms in government that were being attempted with large grants of American foreign aid could improve the basic conditions of the people unless vigorous democratic institutions were built into the nation's local communities through which the population could develop a sense of social and political responsibility. Without an effective program at the community level, the old forces of backwardness and instability would thrive and continue to make many people easy prey for Communist doctrine.

With the advent of Castillo Armas, ambitious plans had been drawn up for national development and despite numerous delays, progress was being made. But the illiterate 75 per cent of the population, having been promised all that heaven has by the previous government under Arbenz, and threatened with abuse if they failed to join Communist organizations, became fearful of reprisals for having had anything to do with the Communists. Unable to comprehend what the revolution meant, except that the world had been suddenly turned around, the nation's peasants simply reverted to their traditional attitude of fatalism.

The change in government had been a necessary condition to the growth of a productive and dynamic society, but without a program of community development such as Moli Stahl had envisaged, it would never be possible to build the local foundations that are essential for such a society, or that are required for the continued growth and maintenance of a progressive national government. Without Moli's kind of a program there could be no assurance that communism would not one day return to Guatemala, despite the government's efforts to prevent it, and no matter how much economic aid might be pumped in at the top by the United States. To improve the basic standards of living, the people had to be provided with personal and practical assistance in the art and practice of democratic action. To fulfill Moli's dream of community development, Castillo Armas offered his personal encouragement.

Moli's plan called for the employment of special workers, trained in democratic organization and leadership, to live and work in the nation's rural communities, generating the quality of civic initiative and action at the local level that would be necessary to make the program work. These workers would be supported by technical and material assistance as needed from the various government agencies in agriculture, health, public works, housing, homemaking, education, and other fields related to community improvement. But essentially it would be a program to encourage and teach the people to think, organize, plan, make decisions, and do things for themselves. In time hundreds of thousands of people throughout the country would become engaged in voluntary citizen efforts to continuously improve their own standards of living and build a working democracy into the social fabric of rural Guatemala.

After discussing the idea with her many friends, especially those in the committee for the blind, she came to feel that a special school to train professional community development workers should be established at the University of San Carlos, Guatemala's national university. Dr. Carlos Martinez Duran, rector of the university, was a scholarly and talented educator who believed that this would be a proper responsibility for the university because it would set in motion a nationwide process to deal effectively with Guatemala's most pressing needs, and would create a flow of information and action between the university, the government, and the people which would grow into a powerful force for the development of a strong nation.

Explaining the idea to her friends, Moli said, "Through this new school we will train full-time people for professional work in community development, but we will also provide a program of field work for all our professions. We want to give all our university students an opportunity to work on solving the social problems of our country instead of just theorizing and organizing public demonstrations."

It was a double-barreled plan for the training of future national leaders and the development of a country.

"The lawyer," she said, "will really know about social legislation because from the time he is a student he will be personally acquainted with the problems of the society. Our graduating engineers and architects will be familiar with the poor people's housing conditions and will develop social vision along with their technical knowledge. Our doctors will develop enough personal concern for the conditions of our rural communities so that not all of them will insist on living in the city. This is a program that can give our sturents a constructive outlet for their energies and their idealism."

Moli formed a committee to begin work on the idea. Her father arranged for the *Fraternidad Quezalteca,* an organization for civic progress of which he was then president, to sponsor promotion of the new school. And then just as the work and planning were getting under way, political upheaval again struck Guatemala.

On July 27, 1957, Castillo Armas was assassinated.

Seven months of national chaos followed. There were two provisional governments, a series of public riots and demonstrations, two elections, charges and counter-charges of election fraud, efforts by the Communists to regain control, and threats of revolution. On March 2, 1958, Miguel Ydígoras, who had served under Castillo Armas as ambassador to Colombia, became the new president of the republic and formed a government pledged to maintain democratic administration.

It was not the most favorable political climate in which to begin the new program, but in her typically aggressive style Moli called on the Ministries of Public Health, Agriculture, Education, the Bank of Quezaltenango, the Bank of Guatemala, the national social security system, and several prominent businessmen for support. In a remarkably short time she obtained pledges from all these groups and raised an initial fund of $25,000, enough to start the new School of Rural Social Service on the branch campus of the University

of San Carlos in Quezaltenango. Moli was appointed the
university's official coordinator to develop the school, a position which she accepted only with the understanding that she
could serve without pay. Julio Hernandez, one of her associates, was employed as the school's full-time director.

They were still short of funds, and struggling to get the
program moving when one evening Moli had as dinner
guests Mr. and Mrs. Al Barrett. A former US State Department official then doing public relations work in Guatemala, Al Barrett knew the country intimately and had great
respect for its people, particularly for the work of Moli
Stahl.

"Why don't you talk to the US foreign aid people about
your rural social service school?" he suggested. "I have a
very good friend by the name of Ray Rignall. . . ."

Moli was ready. A few days later Al Barrett arranged
for the meeting.

Raymond H. Rignall was chief of the *Servicio Coopera-
tivo Interamericano de Educacion,* known as SCIDE, a semi-
autonomous agency established jointly by the governments
of the United States and Guatemala for aid to education. It
operated primarily on joint funds, half from the government
of Guatemala and half from US aid. It was also staffed by
personnel from both governments.

A successful United States public school administrator,
Ray Rignall had entered America's overseas service because people in other lands needed help. To Ray, that was
the way to fight communism, and that was why he was in
foreign aid, not because he wanted to travel, because it
would be an interesting experience, or because it might help
him to acquire added prestige back home. Ray Rignall was
a man with a mission.

He had learned to speak Spanish, and had traveled continuously throughout the country, learning its problems and
making friends. He was looking for innovations to increase
the effectiveness of SCIDE, a characteristic that frequently
brought him into conflict with the complications and formalities of the United States foreign aid organization. But

complications and formalities were not Ray Rignall's primary concern. He worked on the principle that it was his
responsibility to find the best ways of doing his job, whether
those ways were provided in the government manuals or
not; as long as he remained in that frame of mind, conflict
was inevitable. But no one could dispute the fact that he was
making more progress than had ever been made toward better education in Guatemala.

One of Ray's most controversial programs was introduced
over the opposition of some of his superiors. Called community development, it contained the same basic idea that
Moli Stahl was pursuing. The reasoning behind the SCIDE
community development program was contained in a statement by L. A. Berry, one of Ray's associates, which read:
"You cannot develop a good system of education in a country
if simultaneously you do not have progress in other social
and economic institutions, and conversely you cannot develop
and promote the social and economic life of a locality in the
absence of a good system of education."

When Ray arrived in Guatemala he had found a program
called *Socio Educativo Rural* operating as a part of the
Ministry of Education. In this program school teachers had
been given the job of organizing their communities for general self-improvement. The idea of developing local civic
effort had been given major emphasis by Castillo Armas.
But *Socio Educativo Rural* had not produced major results
because the school teachers were too busy teaching school,
and few of them had the necessary experience or training for
community development. Ray had succeeded in getting this
program reorganized so that the teachers were free to teach
school, while other personnel were employed for the community work. It was through the machinery of *Socio Educativo Rural* that Ray was beginning to introduce the
SCIDE community development program.

The United States foreign aid organization in Guatemala,
known as the United States Operations Mission (USOM),
had engaged in highway construction, agricultural projects,
health projects, housing projects, and through SCIDE, in

education projects. There was a project in public administration, a training course in public safety, and an advisory service for industrial management. From all this, many worthwhile projects had been initiated, such as an excellent low cost public housing development in Guatemala City. But like American aid in most countries, the over-all program was in bits and pieces, a project here and a project there. There had been no real comprehensive development of any one community or area of the country, and virtually nothing had been accomplished for the building of local democratic institutions through which the people could engage in civic action and decision-making to change their own living conditions.

It was these gaps that the SCIDE community development program was intended to fill, by organizing the people in selected communities and areas of the country for comprehensive study, planning, and action by the citizens themselves, and by using within the framework of these self-help efforts all relevant services from the USOM, or from the government of Guatemala, or from whatever other sources might be available to bring about the total development of all aspects of a community's life. It was a program that was conceived to cut across all departmental and disciplinary lines in order to bring into play whatever services were needed for a coordinated, unified effort.

Ray and his staff had worked their idea out on paper and had started a few field operations, but that was about as far as they had been able to go. For when Ray Rignall started to put the plan into action he was hit by a veritable explosion of jealousies and red tape from within the United States foreign aid organization.

Other divisions of the USOM in Guatemala accused him of trying to infringe on their territory. Rules and regulations from thick government manuals were thrown up to block his path. SCIDE, they said, should stick to the school business and let each of them stick to its business. Nobody was in the business of community development, and since nobody was interested in that kind of coordination, community development was not a popular term in the USOM.

The objections reverberated all the way to Washington. Finally, Ray Rignall was ordered to quit using the words community development, and to confine the activities of SCIDE a little more strictly to what was generally accepted as education. Then one day Al Barrett walked into Ray Rignall's office and told him he wanted him to meet the most crusading woman in all Guatemala—Señora Elisa Molina de Stahl.

"She's starting a rural social service school in the University of San Carlos," said Al.

Ray's immediate reaction was that he did not know anything about social service, not realizing that in this instance the words social service actually meant community development. But he listened while Al kept insisting he ought to at least look into it.

That afternoon Ray went with Al to a meeting with Moli Stahl. They did not reach agreement at that first meeting. Both of them were practical as well as idealistic. They had to get to know each other. Ray had to be satisfied with the proposed training program. Moli had to be satisfied that Ray really understood Guatemala. They soon realized, however, that they were working for the same goals, and that by combining their efforts a force greater than either of them could be achieved for the development of Guatemala.

Their ideas of community development were virtually identical. As a representative of a foreign government, Ray could not always be in Guatemala. He could give a huge boost toward starting a nationwide program such as he and Moli had in mind, but it had to be continued by concerned Guatemalans.

Moli could go a long way toward providing the concerned Guatemalans and making the program permanent. She could also give a mighty push toward getting it started. But at this point she needed the kind of help that United States foreign aid should be able to provide. Ray and Moli worked out an initial project proposal for $10,000-worth of equipment for the new school to be purchased by SCIDE, but one important obstacle had to be crossed before this proposal could be formally adopted. Could the United States foreign aid agency and the University of San Carlos be brought together to make this project possible?

Not long before, the State Department had officially invited the dean of the university's law school and six other professors to visit the United States. After the invitations had been issued and accepted and the professors were preparing for the trip, United States Embassy representatives had interrogated the dean to such an extent over possible Communist affiliations that he was insulted. News of what had happened swept the campus. All seven of the professors canceled acceptance of their invitations, and hostile attitudes toward the United States hardened within the university. And there had been other incidents. Rector Carlos Martinez Duran had on numerous occasions expressed himself as opposed to the use of United States foreign aid because he was fearful that the acceptance of such aid might jeopardize the independence of the university. The situation was aggravated by the fact that there were foreign aid officials who wanted no part of the university because of alleged Communist infiltration. "We will not work with an institution in which there are Communists," were the words one official had used to sum up the point of view.

But to Moli and Ray the need for the new school and the national program of community development it could help bring about was too great to allow any obstacle to stand in the way. They talked over the situation with the rector. There was no doubt in his mind about the importance of the school and the need for the equipment, and since the aid in this case would be from SCIDE, half the money would be actually Guatemalan. The rector agreed. It was now necessary for a formal request to be issued by the Guatemalan government. Moli followed up on that, and the formal request for SCIDE assistance was issued.

Dedication ceremonies for the official inauguration of the new school were scheduled to be held in Quezaltenango on February 6, 1959. There was to be a formal banquet with the most important dignitaries in all Guatemala, including the rector and other high university officials, leaders from the student organization, prominent private citizens, ministers of government, and even the president of the republic, Miguel Ydígoras. Ray was determined to have the equipment from SCIDE delivered before these ceremonies. He directed his purchasing agents to begin buying immediately, while he proceeded with the necessary paper work.

Everything was moving according to plan. Both Ray and Rector Carlos Martinez Duran were enthusiastic. And then Ray received word that the project would not be approved by the United States foreign aid organization. Ray was dumfounded. He simply could not accept that decision. This was the most promising project he had developed. Weeks passed as he continued to press his argument, and as his purchasing agents kept buying equipment in order to have it ready before the big night in Quezaltenango on February 6. But the approval did not come. Meanwhile, calls were coming in from Quezaltenango wanting to know when the equipment would arrive. Moli was busy using all the influence she could muster to help move through the bottleneck.

Ray was worried. Rector Carlos Martinez Duran was personally interested in this project, and had made it an exception to his position of not asking for United States aid. Moli had gained the interest of many leading faculty members and students. She had obtained the support of some of the most important leaders in government, and some of the country's leading figures in private enterprise. If the $10,000-request were turned down it would not only embarrass SCIDE, it would mean the loss of an unusual opportunity to contribute to the development of Guatemala in a way that carried the approval of some of the most thoughtful leaders in the country.

By this time the SCIDE purchasing machinery was in full operation. Purchasing agents had already bought between four and five thousand dollars-worth of equipment and were pressing their efforts to have the entire order ready for delivery. The agreement with the Guatemalan government had been drawn up in final form and signed by the Guatemalans. All that remained to complete it and thereby release the equipment was the signature of Raymond H. Rignall as the head of SCIDE. But the approval he needed was still not forthcoming.

January 1959 was running out. Plans for the big night in Quezaltenango were moving rapidly. Throughout the nation it was receiving advance coverage in the press. Postponement was unthinkable. A SCIDE truck had been loaded with $10,000-worth of equipment for delivery and was awaiting orders. Moli received an urgent call from Quezaltenango wanting to know if it would be there by Friday, the day of the dedication. She could not bring herself to say the truck might not arrive at all. Ray was considering the necessity of canceling it. The dedication was less than two days away.

He looked at the agreement that he had not been permitted to sign and decided to make one last appeal. Finally, his months of insistence for a program he knew to be sound paid off. Permission was granted and Ray issued orders for the truck to depart.

On the evening of February 6, 1959, the dedication of the new School of Rural Social Service on the branch campus of the University of San Carlos in the old Spanish city of Quezaltenango was one of the most glittering events that had ever taken place in that city. Guests in attendance included everybody from the president of Guatemala on down.

"Until now," said the rector, "had anyone asked what the university is doing for the people of Guatemala, it would have been difficult to say. Now that is changed. This is the most important thing this institution has done in many years."

By the time of its first anniversary, the School of Rural Social Service was firmly established and growing in strength. Sixty students were enrolled in its three-year program. New buildings were being readied for construction under a SCIDE building project, with SCIDE supplying one-third of the cost, the Ministry of Education one-third, and the students and citizens of Quezaltenango supplying the other third in volunteer labor and materials. And SCIDE had approved a $25,000-technical assistance program.

At a national reception in 1960 attended by leading citizens and officials from throughout the nation, Señora Elisa Molina de Stahl was declared Guatemala's Woman-of-the-Year. Among the speakers who honored her, including many of the nation's leading dignitaries, was one of the sixty students enrolled in the new school who said, "She is a woman who understands the pain of the rural man. She has made it possible for us to study a science that teaches us how to understand him, to know him, and to help him overcome his pain. In the style that God loves people is the way this generous lady loves our country."

Then one night a few months later tragedy again struck Guatemala. Raymond H. Rignall died. A man of generosity and known sincerity of purpose, Ray Rignall had gained the friendship and the high respect of people throughout Guatemala. When he died crowds of Guatemalans, as well as North Americans, came to pay their final respects; for he had come to belong to both nations. But it is doubtful that most of those who came to honor him really knew just how great had been their loss. Great ideas and great programs often unknown to the world, but which shape the course of human events, depend upon men of enormous spirit. And sometimes when a great spirit passes, the world never really knows what it has lost. The high goals and generosity of the people of the United States which lie behind their desire to help others and to build an environment for peace in this troubled world may be proclaimed in Washington, in the public press, and from thousands of pulpits across the nation on Sunday. But the realization of those goals will in the final analysis depend upon the extent to which America can set free people like Ray Rignall to go into the world and seek out and join forces with people like Moli Stahl to make way for democracy.

In this tiny nation of tropical Central America with its mountains, jungles, and coastal plains, blessed with natural beauty, but ridden with disease, poverty, and ignorance, the struggle for freedom goes on. In less than thirty years the country has gone through eleven governments, three revolutions, an extreme right-wing dictatorship, a vicious Communist regime, a presidential assassination, scores of public riots, election frauds, and political murders. Three-quarters of the people can neither read nor write. Many still labor to feed their families for less than ten cents a day.

A national program of community development as envisaged by Moli Stahl is the only practical means by which the indigenous effort necessary to change social conditions can be aroused. Thus far the realization of such a program has not been possible, and until this need is sufficiently recognized and acted upon by the government of Guatemala no such program will be possible. Without a national citizens' effort and the exercise of democratic responsibility that such a program mobilizes, there can be no assurance that political upheaval, communism, or another right-wing dictatorship will not return to Guatemala.

This is but one example of the challenge that exists in today's underdeveloped world. It is one of today's tests for the United States with her heritage of democracy and idealism. The United States can meet that test if she can find the Moli Stahls and if she can rise imaginatively and creatively to the opportunities they present.

2
WORLD IN REVOLT

THE ACTIONS OF ANGRY MOBS IN LATIN AMERICA DEMON-strating hostility toward the United States, the precautionary arrests and the mobilization of troops that have been necessary to prevent more such outbursts against visiting United States officials have given dramatic accent to the wave of anti-Yankee feeling that has grown through the years in Latin America.

People in the United States who wonder why such outbursts should occur, who are angered because the Latins are not always convinced of Uncle Sam's sincerity or because they do not always respond with gratitude to Washington offers of aid, should not be misled into believing that this state of affairs is simply a result of Communist influence. Indeed, the Communist agents who have organized to stir hatred and violence throughout Latin America do not deserve even a major share of the credit, for the conditions that have made it possible for the Communists to succeed already existed before they arrived. Through programs of foreign aid, now through the Alliance for Progress, the United States has attempted to help change these conditions, but many barriers are yet to be overcome before the changes that are needed will be brought about.

Latin America, with more than three times the land area of the United States, and with approximately as many people, comprises one of the fastest growing populations in the world. More than seventy million of its people can neither read nor write, and almost that many more are just barely literate. In this vast area conditions range from primitive tribalism to middle-age feudalism to a booming industrial civilization. There is no clear-cut pattern of one thing or the other. Ribbons of steel and concrete provide four-lane express highways across parts of the continent, though most of it is inaccessible; and most of the roads that exist are good only for people on foot, for donkeys, or for travel by jeep.

Brazil, almost as large an area as the United States, has fewer miles of paved highway than the state of Montana. In Mexico City, Bogotá, Caracas, and in many of the other great Latin cities are some of the most modern buildings in the world, some of the finest of residential areas. Yet the overwhelming majority of the people live in primitive grass huts, hovels fashioned of mud, and long stretches of crumbling, stinking, filthy slums. Great industrial factories, the latest in agricultural machinery, and splashes of neon lighting no less spectacular than the Las Vegas Strip are mixed into a land of misery in which peasants plow the ground with sticks, knives, or wooden implements, and in which masses of urban humanity exist through the years without toilets, water, or enough to eat.

In great theatres of art, fashionable hotels, and private drawing rooms, Latin women appear in the latest styles from Paris and New York, while other women go through their lives of toil in little better than rags, wash their clothes in polluted streams, and never see a pair of nylon stockings. It is a land in which the sanctity of the family and moral virtue are held among the highest of values. It is also a land in which the possession of mistresses by refined married gentlemen is often regarded as an expression of masculinity, and in which there are cities where one out of every four women is a practicing prostitute. These problems sometimes become so complex and widespread a part of local custom that moral leaders simply make the decision not to acknowledge the fact that they exist.

In remote jungles and rugged Andean terrain, bands of

armed guerrillas still raid the villages and routes of travel to commit rape, murder, and atrocities, to burn, plunder, and steal. Bodies without heads, the work of machete-wielding bandits, are not uncommon discoveries in places where the army and the police remain helpless to enforce order. On occasion the army and the police have themselves become enemies of the people. Sometimes it has been difficult to determine which is the most dangerous—a soldier, a policeman, or a bandit. One leading Latin put it this way, "Our armies in Latin America have been used for the defeat of our own people."

Great statesmen have come to power, some of whom are in office today, and there are public administrators of scrupulous honesty. But the pattern of politics remains in general a means by which the public office holder gets richer. Public payrolls are a sought-after personal privilege, a route to power and prestige, a form of patronage which makes for a myriad of petty empires, employees that are not needed, and government expenditures for no useful purpose. Taxes are something to avoid. Only a fraction of the taxable wealth has been so much as assessed. Votes remain a commodity to be bought and sold. Coercion is a commonplace part of the election process. Government by revolt and mob rioting is ever present, and political stability remains something for the future.

Government in the Latin countries often presents the outward appearance of a democratic form, but in practice democratic processes receive no more than the barest minimum of attention. Government in most respects neither represents nor adequately serves the majority of the people. Local self-government is yet to be developed, and national government is a highly centralized institution in which the great mass of the people have no voice, and which, from a public service point of view, is remote and unreal. To the majority of the people government is an agent of exploitation, an authority to be feared and avoided.

At the local base of the society, in the villages, the towns, and the neighborhoods of the cities, there is no adequate social or political machinery through which the people may band together to study, to learn, to plan, to work, to form decisions, or to take action to improve their life situation by peaceful means. Nor is there any established means through which new leaders may develop at the local level and rise upward to supply the flow of enlightened leadership that is essential to the building of a dynamic economy and a truly democratic political system. Planning and the determination of policy, the allocation of resources, and the formation of programs for improvement, constitute a business which is limited to the ruling class; the majority of the people have no way of taking part in it or of knowing anything about it.

This void between government and people, between the elite and the masses, is one of the primary reasons why there is so much mass discontent, instability, and violence in the Latin countries, and is one of the major reasons why it is possible for Communist agents to operate so effectively. The Communists seek not only to maintain this void, but to further fragment the society and to engage its various elements in active hostility against each other. These political obstacles to social and economic reform are rooted in a system of class, caste, and social inequality which began with European conquest in the sixteenth century and which to this day forces the vast majority of Latin Americans to trudge and suffer through an average life span of less than thirty-five years under the burden of indescribable poverty, disease, and insecurity. Most of the cultivated land is owned by relatively few, while the majority are either landless or own plots so small that anything more than bare existence is impossible. Overlaying the masses like a blanket of iron, and profiting from their plight, is the traditional oligarchy of the landlords, the *patróns,* the rich, and the politically powerful.

The Alliance for Progress has sought to change these conditions by attaching certain reform requirements to United States economic aid. But these conditions will not be changed by any form of economic aid until an organizational machinery is established within the public administration of the Latin governments by which the people, the elite and the masses together, can understand and correct their social and political deficiencies. Widely based popular respect for democratic processes and abhorrence of totalitarianism must be generated, but this can be accomplished only if a mechanism is established through which the great mass of the population is involved in decision-making and given a significant role in the job of nation-building, and if all legitimate elements in the society are mobilized and actively united in the effort. Only if this kind of social and political machinery is organized and activated will it be possible to bring about an atmosphere of political order in which significant social and economic progress can be achieved, in which the challenge of revolution can be met, and in which the Communists can be denied their opportunity for subversion.

The concept of community development that Moli Stahl attempted to introduce in Guatemala is an essential step toward achieving these ends. Carrying out this idea, if done on a nationwide scale, would make it possible to build into the local communities democratic institutions through which the masses and the elite could mount an effective joint effort for their common good. With this kind of institutional machinery, foreign aid as well as the vast resources within Latin America itself could be utilized effectively.

In recent years considerable interest in the concept of community development has been growing in many countries in Latin America. Along with that interest there has arisen a new desire for a life abundant for all the people, and a slow realization of the social and political responsibility that must be assumed by men and women of good will if tomorrow's great potential is to be achieved. This new spirit has not yet emerged sufficiently to overcome the obstructions which still make it impossible to realize that potential, but a ferment of determination to improve the common welfare has now reached the point where national programs of community development could be successfully instituted if the kind of leadership and understanding exemplified by Ray Rignall were forthcoming from United States foreign aid.

In the strange mixture that is Latin America there is a

tradition of human charity, warmth, and sincerity of purpose. There is a burning nationalism, and a patriotism that leads men to perform the heroic. There is a high intelligence, an ability for leadership, and a will to respond through the mobilization of effort on the part of the people. There is a high moral tone, a feeling of spirituality and dedication, unsurpassed by any other people in the world. Nowhere does the desire for justice and democracy cry out more vehemently. Nowhere are the people more likable.

These qualities, so often buried in the morass of corruption, injustice, and political immaturity that have held back the development of an advanced civilization for centuries, stand in sharp relief against the background of contradiction, paradox, and confusion that is Latin America. Yet here in this vast region are all the resources, human and physical, for the building of a truly great and democratic society if a system for that purpose, such as was envisaged by Moli Stahl in Guatemala, could be established as an integral part of the public administration in every Latin country.

The new spirit of progress that is beginning to emerge in this world in revolt is coming from many sources, one of the most important of which are the Latin American universities. From these institutions a new class of intellectuals has come into being, people who are as interested in politics and social reform as they are in academic studies, people who are restless to take action against the depressed standards of living, but who need guidance to get started. Such people are not always certain of their direction, but they want to go somewhere other than where they are now. Within them there is deep resentment toward what they have seen as an ancient pattern of injustice exercised by the landlords, the patróns, and the political figures who have become dictators.

From these universities has come much of the political fervor that in recent times has influenced the direction of governments, sparked public riots and demonstrations, and at times even helped to ignite revolutions. Because of this, the Latin universities have been scheduled as prime targets for Communist infiltration, and many of them are among the chief purveyors of anti-North American sentiment. This does not mean that the universities of Latin America are "hotbeds of communism," as many people have alleged. It only means that within these institutions there is an acute sensitivity to the region's social and economic ills, and a deep-seated desire to see these conditions changed. Recognizing this as a strategic opportunity for their own purposes, the Communists are attempting to use the universities as instruments through which to press their campaigns of agitation and unrest, while other workers interested in the cause of democracy and solid national development have tended to avoid them. Thus, the new class of intellectuals, much of which is arising from the universities, can be viewed either as a new hope for the future, or as a potential new danger, depending upon the degree to which its aspirations for better social conditions find satisfaction through constructive methods. Thus far, little has been done to initiate programs of community development aimed at constructive social change that would provide the idealists among university students with an outlet for their social ambitions.

Many of the new class, both inside and outside the universities, are driven by a hostility toward anything that might symbolize power or wealth that they do not have, and which they feel should somehow be used for the benefit of all the people. It is one of the signs of the times, a stirring among idealists, an expression of the inner feelings of aggression and the militancy that throughout human history has come to the surface wherever men have begun to reach out for freedom and self-determination not yet fully attained. In some ways it is the age-old argument of the have-nots against the haves, with the wealthy United States becoming the epitome of the haves. This whole stirring, coupled with a long shadow of United States domination in the Latin American economy and pre-eminence in hemispheric politics, has placed the United States in a highly vulnerable position for criticism. Instead of meeting this situation with imaginative support and encouragement for programs that would enable orderly change to be achieved and thereby help dry up the criticism, the United States foreign aid agency has been little more than a technician and money-lender. This failure to operate with an attitude of human warmth and willingness to adjust to other people's ideas—while still retaining firm principles of good business administration which obviously must accompany the lending of public money—has only added to the difficulties in developing the kind of indigenous activities that are essential if the aid funds are to be used effectively in the cause of freedom.

In the family of the Americas, Uncle Sam is looked upon as the rich uncle, and like most rich uncles who exercise heavy influence in family affairs, is revered in some ways and feared in others. In the eyes of many Latins, he has plenty for himself and for everybody else in the family as well. Also, like most rich uncles he never does quite what the family wishes, and when he does he is frequently resented for the way he does it. He is particularly resented when he holds out his checkbook for the purpose of buying the family's good will.

Moreover, on the basis of past performance which only recently has been changed, the Latins acquired a habit of looking upon the great ado over the willingness of Uncle Sam to spend money for aid to their countries as somewhat academic. During the fifteen years following the end of World War II, they never hesitate to point out, the United States spent fifty times as much in Europe and Asia as it did among its fellow family members. This, they feel, was because Uncle Sam did not consider them sufficiently important for his purposes, and that only when they became threatening did he begin to pay any particular attention to them.

This attitude was dramatically illustrated by the reaction of the Latins to an announcement from the Eisenhower administration in the summer of 1960 of a special $500 million-aid fund for Latin America. After years of urging from the Latin governments, many leading Latins said this was the first time the United States had offered any substantial aid for social purposes. Officially, most Latin diplomats at the Bogotá Conference of Foreign Ministers in September 1960, where plans were discussed for the administration of the fund, were deeply grateful and full of praise for this gesture of understanding from their rich neighbor to the north. But outside the conference hall the special United States aid fund was widely referred to as the "Castro Plan."

"They would never have done it had Fidel Castro not forced them into it," was the public reaction I heard in Bogotá. And although most Latins had by that time lost sympathy for Castro, many applauded him for what they saw as an act of courage in standing up to Uncle Sam and making him take heed of his neighbors to the south. The reasoning as to the United States motive for taking new interest in Latin America was, of course, correct.

Said one United States editorial, typical of many, "The Cuban revolutionary dictator, Fidel Castro, has inadvertently done the other American republics a favor. By showing how communism can come to this hemisphere, he has finally awakened the United States to the need for a Marshall Plan for Latin America designed to demonstrate the advantages of cooperation with the free world as opposed to the Communists."

To the Latins the help was sorely needed. The situation was, and will long continue to be, pretty desperate. Yet many were resentful over the idea that they were being helped only because of the situation created by Castro. This same fear of a Castro revolution is becoming increasingly prevalent in the Latin power elite, and among most of its members is a major incentive for whatever action they might be willing to take to improve the lot of their own peasant classes. But it is always difficult for one receiving aid from his rich uncle to appreciate the uncle when he feels he is getting the aid only because the uncle expects a favor in return. This applies particularly to the rising new class which holds as much suspicion toward its own power elite as it does toward Uncle Sam.

United States diplomatic representatives appear to have

been remarkably successful at getting most of the hemispheric delegates to vote according to United States wishes at most inter-American conferences. But this does not mean that the United States has enjoyed the devotion and respect of the Latins. From the viewpoint of many Latins, particularly those of the idealistic new class who are exerting an increasing influence on public opinion, the United States is big, powerful, smug, complacent, materialistic, and selfish. The extent of this feeling was deeply impressed upon me when I heard one South American high in the social and economic ranks of his country express the attitude this way: "The great danger of communism is in the United States because you people have no real spiritual values to govern your lives or to fight for. Your prime values are material. How can you expect us to be comfortable under that kind of leadership?"

The image of the United States as seen by the Latins may not be the image of North America as seen by her own people, and in fact does not represent a fair or accurate judgment. Yet it is urgent that citizens of the United States bear in mind the long history of Latin complaints and not react to these criticisms childishly or resentfully; instead they must try realistically to understand the impression their country has made upon other people in the Western Hemisphere. And it would be well to realize, too, that there is considerable basis for the hostile attitudes which have been growing in Latin America. When a country becomes as powerful and as wealthy as the United States in contrast with its neighbors, and when that country sets itself up as the model of democracy in the free world, then that country should not be surprised if it becomes a target of criticism.

For many years there was widespread resentment in Latin America toward what the Latins regarded as a United States policy of supporting dictators. Official United States spokesmen repeatedly denied this, but these denials did not alter the Latins' belief. They pointed to Venezuela's Jiménez, to Somoza in Nicaragua, Peron in Argentina, Rojas Pinilla in Colombia, Batista in Cuba, Trujillo in the Dominican Republic, and others who were said to have received support and comfort from the United States government over the objection of local citizens. Many Latins still contend that United States support was extended to these and other governments that were considered corrupt for the sole purpose of benefiting United States financial interests.

In January 1960, José Figueres, former president of Costa Rica and still an important opinion leader in Latin America, said to me, "How can those of us who are attempting to foster understanding toward the United States succeed when the United States insists on keeping these despots in power? The official attitude of your government," he said, "seems to be that democracy is a necessary nuisance at home, but if you can do without it abroad so much the better."

These attitudes have run deeply, and have not been limited to a few people. Somehow, whether true or not, they represent important impressions of the United States that are widespread in the Latin world. At the San José conference of the Organization of American States in August 1960 the United States joined with most of the Latin countries in officially condemning Dictator Trujillo in the Dominican Republic and thus made some advance toward overcoming the onus of being a supporter of dictators. But again many people in Latin America were not impressed, for in their interpretation this was merely a form of political log rolling. At that conference, many Latins pointed out, the United States wanted support for a resolution against Castro.

"We don't like Castro any better than you do," a prominent Latin told me, "but if the United States is really the leader of democracy in this hemisphere why did you wait for us to take the initiative in introducing a resolution against Trujillo?"

Many Latin idealists believe that wealthy business interests in the United States have been working in collaboration with the Latin oligarchy to maintain control over the masses for the benefit of their mutual economic interests. Today some of these attitudes may seem far-fetched, particularly in view of the definite attitude the United States government has assumed against dictators and the policy of good citizenship which has developed among most United States private companies. But as long as such attitudes exist they will continue to contribute to the forces that would destroy democracy in all the Americas, including the United States; and foreign aid has not yet begun to operate in a manner that would effectively overcome these attitudes.

Latins are incensed at the existence of racial prejudice in the United States even though there is far less social equality in their countries than there is in North America. But they point out that this is a form of hypocrisy which reveals a national insincerity toward the concept of human rights in the country that calls itself the world's greatest advocate of this concept.

The extreme vulnerability of the United States to criticism is reflected in the many Latin complaints that frequently border on pettiness, and which in some respects seem to have become a kind of phobia. They even resent the use of the term "American" by citizens of the United States on the grounds that North Americans are no more entitled to the use of the name "American" than are Latin Americans. Technically, of course, they are right, but there is nothing to be gained by explaining that this name has been applied to residents of the United States over many generations and has come into general world usage. Another example of pettiness was the reaction in 1960 that followed the argument over flying the Panamanian flag along with the United States flag at the Panama Canal. After months of agitation which was kept boiling by radical extremists, the United States complied with the Panamanian request only to find that certain Panamanians were still disgruntled on the grounds that their flag had not been placed in a sufficiently conspicuous location.

Other sources of irritation relate to what Latins have long viewed as a superior attitude within the United States foreign aid organization. Many Latins contend that United

States technicians have often acted as though they were better and smarter than the "natives," and, according to the Latins, refuse to listen to advice on what is most needed or how a given project should be conducted. This, it is said, has frequently resulted in the waste of both United States and Latin funds. United States government employees are seen by many Latins who deal with them daily as people who are more interested in following their Washington manuals and regulations than they are in solving problems. Feelings such as these make for lively conversation when Latin Americans gather among themselves, and help keep alive an attitude that the United States is not really as interested in promoting the welfare of others as it says it is.

These irritations, whether a result of fact or fancy, are given added weight by such projects as a one-thousand bed hospital built under United States foreign aid to serve a pressing need for medical care, but which came to be looked upon as a landmark to Yankee attitudes of superiority. When I visited this great hospital in 1960 it had operated for more than two years at only half capacity because of delays in the delivery of equipment; local citizens were understandably resentful because across town in an old, poorly equipped, and overcrowded hospital patients were sleeping on the floor, and two and three sick children were being put into the same bed. No amount of explanation for such a situation can overcome the unfavorable public opinion it engenders toward the United States, and even though this health facility was badly needed it made little, if any, contribution toward the cultivation of a democratic, self-sufficient society.

These are samples of the many irritations growing out of foreign aid that have added to anti-North American attitudes and played into the hands of the enemies of freedom despite the large sums of United States capital that have been fed into Latin America. Much of the hostility is based on a long-standing prejudice and a current lack of accurate information. In many instances it is the result of rumor and misinterpretation. But there have been cases where it was just, and the general atmosphere has been so sensitive that it supports hostile attitudes whether they spring from gossip or fact. The important thing is that these attitudes, right or wrong, exist and are continuously fanned and exploited by skilled Communist agitators and other extremists.

Everywhere in Latin America the campaign of Communist dogma is being speeded up. It is a problem that has been coming on for many years and there is no easy way out. The solution is not so much a matter of fighting communism as it is in mobilizing the forces of democracy for an effective attack on the prevailing conditions that present the Communists with their opportunity for success. Human misery, inequality, and the rising idealism of Latin America have made conditions ripe for the infusion of communism. These same conditions represent an equally great opportunity to demonstrate what can be accomplished for man's welfare by the forces of democracy. Only by an approach in which the defeat of communism becomes a by-product of changes that are induced in the process of making democracy work can communism be effectively stopped.

But by what means do you mobilize the forces of democracy? What is it that has to be built to make democracy work? Certainly you do not mobilize the forces of democracy simply by pouring in capital or by lending money, even though requirements of social and economic reform are attached to the loans. Such reforms cannot be accomplished simply because a government agrees to them and offers a plan that qualifies it as eligible for the loan. The Latins are past masters at maneuvering themselves into a better bargaining position with Uncle Sam by drawing up plans which never quite get carried out. Democracy can not be made into a dynamic working force by simply building *things*—hospitals, bridges, roads, factories, irrigation systems, or any other physical amenities. To make democracy a reality and to release its power for human welfare in Latin America, something else must be built; namely, organizational machinery that will enable the great mass of the people to

exert their own initiative, honestly engage themselves in the
nation-building process, become in fact a participating people, and join their efforts with those of the government so
that all groups within the society may unite and work together to carry out the changes that are needed for the
social, economic, and political advancement of their country.

The concept of community development, properly introduced and carried out on a nationwide scale, will provide
the machinery, the stimulation and motivation, the coordination and the unity necessary to carry out this approach by
actually making it possible for democracy to work. Community development conceived and implemented for this broad
political purpose offers the only practical means through
which United States aid can be utilized with maximum
benefit to Latin America while at the same time generating
the desired mutual friendship and understanding between
the peoples and the governments of the Americas.

The creative thinking of Moli Stahl and Ray Rignall in
Guatemala has illustrated some of the important attributes
of community development. Colombia, which has gone
further than any other country on the South American continent to initiate a national community development program, further illustrates these attributes. The example
provided by Colombia is important not so much for what it
has accomplished, but for what can be learned from what is
not yet accomplished. As in virtually all of Latin America,
Colombia has all the ingredients for successful community
development: the human energy, the ideas, and the physical
resources. It has everything except the unity and the organizational machinery that are required to combine these
elements into an effective operation.

In 1958, a law was passed directing the Colombian government to encourage the people to undertake self-help
projects for the improvement of their living conditions. This
law did not accomplish much, but it did help to popularize the
idea of self-help and *acción comunal,* or community action.
In 1959, President Alberto Lleras Camargo issued a decree
calling for the creation of a Division of Community Action

within the government, and ordered all nation-building agencies to cooperate. Within a short time, virtually every government agency began labeling almost everything it did *acción comunal,* as bureaucrats and politicians scurried about to be counted in under the provisions of the decree. All over the country the peasants (*campesinos*) who comprise the bulk of Colombia's population were prodded into building roads, aqueducts, latrines, and other physical projects that were regarded by government functionaries as beneficial.

A few months later the most powerful private organization in the country, the National Federation of Coffee Growers, voted to allocate fifty million pesos per year (about $7 million) to expand a program of rural aid which the federation was already carrying on in the coffee-producing areas of the country. The fifty million pesos was an amount which was returned to the federation by the government from the proceeds of a coffee export tax with the understanding that the federation would use it for the benefit of the coffee-producing peasants.

At this point the international relief organization, CARE, through its enterprising mission chief, Mary Lowrie, began working with the coffee federation and the government to help forward what then appeared to be a potential move toward a national community development program. CARE realized that such a program would make it possible to increase greatly the effectiveness of its distributions of tools and other self-help materials to Colombian villages, and therefore began a concerted effort to bring such a program into being. This effort added greatly to the enthusiasm, and over a period of months meetings were held almost daily to try to work out a national program that would create a working partnership between the government, the coffee federation, and all other major groups in the country, including the Roman Catholic Church which embraces over 90 per cent of all Colombians. CARE conducted a comprehensive nationwide survey, the only one of its kind that had ever been done in Latin America, to pinpoint the country's assets for a national community development program, and it even arranged a trip for a Colombian delegation to inspect a similar program established some years before in the Philippines.

But despite the interest that was generated and the plans that were made, more than a year passed with the Colombians taking no real action to bring a national community development program into being. It was a period to which one person referred as *"plan sí, acción no!"* In rural areas across the country, thousands of physical improvements were made, but little was done to stimulate democratic community organization, educate citizens for self-determination, or bridge the gap between the masses and the ruling elite. Not much was done to unite the many divided elements in the society, or to replace suspicion and discontent with trust and new hope, and there was virtually no coordination among the official services.

There was, in short, no real community development. Indeed, with the exception of a few leaders, the actual goal of the work being done in the rural areas was not the development of democratic communities, but the development of public works with peasant labor which, under the patriotic banner of *acción comunal,* could be had for nothing. Few people had any idea of what the concept of community development meant. In its paper implications the presidential decree for community action was a sweeping document for the mobilization of the nation's resources. But it did not produce a national community development program because it did not provide the administrative machinery and the citizens' organization necessary to make such a program possible.

During this period the capital city of Bogotá was astir with meetings and conversations accenting the urgency for a national program that could quell the widespread peasant discontent which many leaders interpreted as threats of a social uprising. Only recently the country had emerged from twelve years of civil war during which approximately 300,000 people had been killed. Now violence was again spreading in the mountainous countryside, and Communist infiltration was growing. In the face of these fears, a group of prominent Colombian business and professional leaders organized a private effort to help support the community development idea and hasten the formation of a nationwide program. They retained a private North American consultant, Gabriel L. Kaplan, who had helped organize the national community development program in the Philippines, to help devise and implement the program in Colombia.

Through this private group a comprehensive development plan was proposed in which all nation-building services of the government, the coffee federation, and other non-governmental interests would coordinate their work in a single nationwide operation in which people in peasant villages throughout the country would become actively involved. The plan called for technical advisors and a wide range of material assistance to be made available in response to specific requests from the village people and delivered to them through a citizens' development organization to be established in each village. Field organizers given special training and carefully selected from the nation's universities, where there was a surplus of discontented but able young people, were to be sent out to help get the citizens' organizations established and activated.

Through this plan, democratic thought and action were to be infused into the roots of the nation, and the population mass was to be taught to make decisions and take constructive action for its own improvement with the help of the government and all other pro-democratic forces in the country. Through a national community development administrative machinery which would employ the field organizers and coordinate the supporting work of all national agencies—private and governmental—this program would become the primary basis for planning the national budget so that the entire Colombian citizenry—masses and elite alike—would be given a significant role in shaping the operations of government, providing, as a by-product, a powerful deterrent to communism.

This plan was endorsed in principle by the president of the republic, and by a number of other leading Colombians who felt that a genuine working democracy was the only salvation for their country and for Latin America. But thus far no action has been taken to adopt this or any other realistic plan to make democracy a national possibility.

After numerous delays the government implemented its Division of Community Action to help coordinate development work. The coffee federation established a social and economic department through which it has trained and employed more than fifty community workers to help village peasants engage in local improvement projects. And there are many other efforts aimed at encouraging village improvement, including a massive national radio program led by a Catholic priest, Monsignor José Joaquin Salcedo. Meanwhile, CARE has greatly expanded its self-help activities, and in 1961 was instrumental in bringing in a unit of Peace Corps volunteers to encourage community development activities in the villages. Despite inadequate material support, the contribution of these volunteers has been so outstanding that a few months after their arrival the Colombian government asked the Peace Corps to send a second unit, which at this writing is in the process of being assembled.

In no other Latin American country is more attention being given to the job of relieving the misery of the masses than in Colombia. But until a national program for a working political democracy is adopted, the current efforts being made will not result in substantial alteration in the conditions that make Colombia, along with the rest of Latin America, a ripe field for Communist penetration, and in all too many respects, a wasteland for United States foreign aid.

The situation is made even more serious by the fact that the same critical conditions prevail in virtually all other parts of the underdeveloped world. In country after country there is the familiar ruling class, the insufferable poverty of the masses. Not only is there no way for the majority of the people to be included in the political processes of their country, there is no means by which they can even be made aware of what their government is doing or of any hope to attain, peacefully, a decent standard of living in their lifetimes.

As I moved from Latin America to the Middle East and on through Asia and the Orient, I began to realize just how much the world is turning from the past and taking on new forms. Just what these new forms will be, I would not care to predict; but there can be no doubt that a powerful social revolution is now gathering momentum around the globe, and that before it is finished we will have a very different kind of world than we have now. In all of the newly developing countries the established systems that have held the masses in check are beginning to crack. Everywhere there is an impelling urge to see conditions changed and a relentless Communist effort to take advantage of the situation. Anyone who doubts that this is true or who would dismiss the Communist menace as an overworked phrase is simply blinding himself to the possible day when freedom-loving people may be confronted by an accumulation of hostility unlike anything the world has known since the hordes of Genghis Khan swept over Asia.

As the clamor for a better life continues to mount, the gap between desire and reality continues to widen. Everywhere people are demanding a larger share of the benefits of the modern age, but in most countries the social and political structures by which economic resources could be used effectively are absent. Thus, the level of aspiration of the underdeveloped world continues to rise; the ability to obtain its fulfillment by peaceful means is proportionately decreased; and the inevitable result is a piling up of human frustrations, a heightening of tensions, and a potential explosion of emotional pressures.

It is this situation not only in Latin America, but in all underdeveloped areas of the globe, that is providing the basis for a threat to world freedom which has made foreign aid a modern necessity. But unless operations can be established that will make this aid more effective than it has been, mankind may well witness either the destruction of the human race or the beginning of a second dark age. Never in history has man been so confronted by so staggering a backlog of human needs and so horrible a threat to the survival of freedom.

This problem cannot be solved simply by diplomatic means, by loans and grants no matter how large, or by a kind of foreign aid aimed solely at physical improvements. Man's physical needs are too vast and overwhelming. Moreover, the meeting of physical needs, important as it is, does not mean that the cause of freedom has been furthered. Both the Russians and the Chinese Communists are advancing in physical achievements. The development of values within a social and political structure that will permit the exercise of popular will and determination in an atmosphere of freedom must go hand in hand with any technical or economic advance, if this advance is to contribute to the dignity of man and a world environment of peace.

All over the world American foreign aid has focused on the building of roads, dams, irrigation systems, compost pits, latrines, houses, water lines, health centers, bath houses, schools, and every other kind of physical improvement that can be imagined. It has built everything but communities and democratic societies. And while all this building has been going on—a job which could have been better accomplished by battalions of Seabees—while the flow of money has increased, the world climate for freedom has steadily deteriorated, and the forces of social unrest and regimentation have moved forward.

If the battle for democracy is to be won by peaceful means, the underdeveloped world must be supplied with positive leadership and assistance in programs that will reach directly into the millions of local communities where people live, cultivate within them qualities of self-reliance, engage them in an organized effort of their own, create a nationwide sense of mutual confidence between government and people, and organize public administration in a manner that will accommodate these ends. Aid is needed that will enable the masses to organize and enrich their lives that they may rise up from their present miserable environment and mold a new environment to satisfy their own needs and wishes. Properly conducted programs of community development can answer the call for help with programs which foster the growth of freedom and the exercise of democratic processes, meeting the physical and social needs of the underdeveloped world.

But this call has too long gone unanswered, and time is running short. The people of the United States have devoted large quantities of foreign aid to military and economic matters. They have supplied money and technicians in abundance. But American foreign aid has yet to make an adequate response to the needs of the underdeveloped world in terms of the social and political dimensions of the problem; until it does, the economic needs will not be met. It has yet to recognize the importance of a Moli Stahl, or to understand that all too few Raymond H. Rignalls have been present at the scene of action.

3

THE BUREAUCRATS

ON JANUARY 20, 1949, MORE THAN A HUNDRED THOUSAND Americans stood in front of the capitol in Washington, D. C., to hear the inaugural address of Harry S. Truman and to cheer the beginning of his second term as President of the United States.

"Each period of our national history has its special challenges," he said.

"Those that confront us now are as momentous as any in the past. Today marks the beginning not only of a new Administration, but of a period that will be eventful, perhaps decisive, for us and for the world.

"It may be our lot to experience, and in large measure to bring about, a major turning point in the long history of the human race. . . ."

The President of the United States was about to announce a significant new addition to America's policy of extending aid to a misery-infested world.

"In the coming years," he said, "our program for peace and freedom will emphasize four major courses of action.

"First, we will continue to give unfaltering support to the United Nations and related agencies. . . ." His second point was to continue the European economic recovery program which had been extended to certain other areas, and the third was to "strengthen freedom-loving nations against the dangers of aggression."

Then came his famous fourth point. "We must embark on a bold new program for making the benefits of our scientific advances and industrial progress available for the improvement and growth of underdeveloped areas. . . . It must be a worldwide effort for the achievement of peace, plenty and freedom."

A new effort, soon to become famous as Point Four, had been proclaimed. Through this "bold new program," America was to use her storehouse of knowledge to help more than half the people on earth lift themselves to a higher standard of living within the framework of a free society. It was a far-sighted effort intended to help create a world environment in which mankind could live in peace. This was America's response to the problems of the underdeveloped world. It was one of the greatest acts of generosity and responsible leadership by any nation in human history. But in actual operation, the bureaucracy created to administer the program has not been equal to the goals for which the program was intended.

In September 1950, the Technical Cooperation Administration (TCA) was created within the State Department to assume responsibility for carrying out the new program. In Europe, the Far East, and in certain parts of Southeast Asia the program was handled by the Economic Cooperation Administration (ECA) which had been created in 1948 to administer the Marshall Plan. In Latin America, it was the responsibility of the Institute for Inter-American Affairs, a government corporation that was attached to the newly created TCA. In 1951, the ECA was abolished and the Mutual Security Agency (MSA) was created to take its place, but with the TCA still operating from the State Department. Two years later the MSA and the TCA were both abolished and their functions, along with those of the Institute for Inter-American Affairs, were unified into a new independent agency, the Foreign Operations Administration (FOA). In 1955, the FOA was abolished and its functions transferred to a newly created, semi-autonomous agency within the State Department, the International Cooperation Administration (ICA). Thus Point Four was back in the State Department where it had started in the first place, though operated directly by ICA, an almost independent agency.

By this time many people were confused. Within five years after it started, Point Four had been involved in one way or another with seven government agencies; and as one official put it, "the operating instructions and internal organization were changing almost from week to week." But America was going through a new experience: an attempt to develop national economies by democratic methods in countries lacking the traditions and institutions that make it possible for democracy to function.

The problem of helping the underdeveloped world is quite different from that encountered in Europe during the operations of the Marshall Plan. In Europe it was simply a matter, vast in magnitude, of supplying the means by which people of high technical competence could rebuild an economy that had existed only a few years before but which had been destroyed by war. In the underdeveloped countries, many of which had just been born as independent nations, it was a matter of starting a development that had never before existed, in lands in which there was no political or social mechanism through which the vast majority of the people could take part in the effort. Here there were few people in a position to make decisions concerning their own lives. There were millions who were unhappy and dissatisfied, but they did not know what to do to change their situation, and they were seriously suspicious of government. In these countries the national public administration was not organized and did not function in a way that would make government responsive to the needs and desires of the people, or that would encourage in them the confidence that was necessary to cause them to make the changes which progress demanded.

This was not a job for which modern America was prepared, certainly not the United States government. However, ten years and billions of dollars later, a vast program

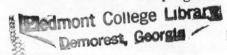

of foreign aid aimed at the underdeveloped world had jelled into a typical Washington bureaucracy within the huge and complex organization of the International Cooperation Administration. Headed by an administrator who reported to the mutual security coordinator in the State Department, the ICA was roughly divided into two major branches: operations, which handled the administration of programs; and technical services, which supplied technical advice to the administration. In countries throughout the world where the program operated there was a foreign aid mission, known officially as the United States Operations Mission, or USOM. Each USOM was headed by a director who occupied a position among United States employees second only to the ambassador. In some countries the USOM director frequently enjoyed even more prestige than the ambassador because of the large staff he controlled, and because in many countries the host government had grown dependent upon foreign aid funds as a routine part of its own national budget.

A USOM was in some respects like a government within a government. It was one of the most important public offices in the country, well known to all public officials, and in many respects casting the shadow of a foreign giant over all activities of the national government. It was looked upon with feelings of awe, respect, friendliness, disgust, fear, resentment, and as a place where many of the local people could get a better job than they ever had before. In many countries, few major decisions were made by the national government without first checking the attitude of USOM, though in many instances it was politely listened to and then ignored.

Each USOM was divided into a series of divisions, each having responsibility for one or more operating programs, such as programs in agriculture, education, public health, transportation. All USOM division chiefs were under the supervision of the mission director, and officially, most communications between the mission and Washington were sent through his office. The mission director exercised great influence in determining program plans, and in determining what new divisions would or would not be established in his USOM. But the attitude of the major USOM division chiefs exerted a powerful influence upon mission policy, and upon the attitudes and actions of the mission director. New program proposals were, of course, subject to Washington approval, a process which was extremely slow and tedious, and which was based not merely upon the broad policy of the President of the United States, but also upon the professional prejudices within the bureaucracy which often operated to thwart the policies of the President and the intent of Congress.

The decisions as to what programs a USOM was to support were theoretically based upon the requests of the host government; but many techniques were used to cause the host government to request those services that the USOM wished to render; and in many instances, attempts were made to shape a country's program without sufficient regard for its indigenous culture and peculiar needs. These situations, always fraught with friction and misunderstanding, inevitably led to unfortunate attitudes toward the United States, thereby introducing needless strains into the foreign aid operation. None of the nations in which ICA was working appreciated being treated as an object of charity or of being made to feel that a foreign power was dictating its life, and wherever a USOM was able to get its way only by irritating the members of the host government, the whole purpose of Point Four was defeated.

If a healthy working partnership was established between the officials and personnel of the two governments, and if USOM leadership was creative and imaginative, it was possible for USOM to exercise great influence to the mutual advantage of both countries. The major test of USOM leadership was whether it resulted in programs that most effectively met the needs of the country, rather than programs that simply reflected the established professional routine and habits of the Americans. With its wide experience in many countries throughout the world, ICA was in a unique position to act as a catalyst for the spread of new ideas if it avoided the weakness of being bound by professional interests or bureaucratic jealousies at home so as to preclude the possibility of accepting new ideas.

Ordinarily, the USOM did not work directly with the people its programs were designed to reach, because it did not actually operate programs. The programs it supported were usually carried out by officials and employees of the host government, by organizations designated for that purpose by the host government, or by third parties contracted by the two governments. USOM merely furnished material and financial support and supplied technicians who acted as advisors to the host government officials. Thus, the operations of USOM were conducted on a government-to-government basis.

The technical service branch of ICA in Washington supplied advice to the USOM's throughout the world, but had no direct control over program operations. However, some of the technical service offices occupied positions of high status in the ICA hierarchy that made it possible for them to exercise powerful influence over what programs were to be established in the various countries being aided. Thus, one of the prime considerations as to what programs were introduced in a given country was not necessarily the conditions that prevailed in the country, but the professional interests of influential ICA offices, without sufficient thought being given to the readiness of the people in the underdeveloped country to make appropriate use of the skills the professional technicians had to offer.

One of the largest and most influential ICA technical services was the Office of Food and Agriculture, and one of the smallest and least influential was the Community Development Division. Indeed, the Community Development Division was so insignificant a part of the bureaucracy that many people in the ICA were hardly aware of its existence. Others, particularly in the Office of Food and Agriculture, wished it were not there, viewing it as a threat to their piece of the bureaucratic empire. This view was shared by other ICA officials in such offices as education and public health who were always striving to obtain increased status for their units and who were opposed to the comprehensive approach of community development.

From the earliest days of Point Four the foreign aid program was heavily influenced by officials representing agricultural extension, a system in the United States designed to convey to American farmers the latest information about farming from laboratories and experiment stations. The assumption was automatic that, inasmuch as the need for increased food production was a universal problem in the underdeveloped countries, and inasmuch as the great majority of the people in these countries lived in rural villages and eked out what little sustenance they had by primitive methods, a supply of experts who could teach modern farming methods would be an obvious way to achieve the goals of Point Four. Because of this assumption, and because of the fact that agricultural extension in the United States represented a political system of considerable power, large numbers of agricultural technicians were brought into the Point Four operations, and much of the foreign aid effort in the underdeveloped countries was directed in accordance with the professional interests of these technicians.

Insufficient recognition was given the fact that agricultural extension in the United States evolved under vastly different social, economic, and political circumstances than those prevailing in the Middle East, Asia, Africa, and Latin America, where the democratic institutions essential to a dynamic economy were yet to be formed. In the United States agricultural extension had been an integral part of a great era of free, private initiative, flowering and bursting on a scale no other part of the world has ever witnessed. The advance of agriculture in America was due to many factors, partly commercial and economic, but the primary factor was the existence of a democratic system which made it possible for farmers to organize for educational purposes and to exercise a degree of initiative which the lack of a democratic system had made impossible in the underdeveloped countries.

The whole culture of these countries was utterly different

from anything most Americans had ever heard of, and was neither socially nor politically suited to the highly specialized system of agricultural extension. The vast majority of the people in these countries were illiterate, and had no past experience that would persuade them to adopt the methods of modern agriculture unless they were regimented, as in the Communist countries, or unless they were led through a type of democratic social and political development which would make it possible for them to exercise their powers of free thought, decision-making, and local initiative. They could hardly be expected to jump from the stone age to the mid-twentieth century just because a former county agent from Kansas told an official of their national government how to grow better wheat. Nor would a carbon copy of the United States system of state agricultural colleges and experiment stations make the jump easier.

These were lands in which millions of peasants had never seen a hoe and worked plots of land no larger than a small city lot. In most countries a few wealthy landlords owned most of the land under cultivation, and in some places such as the Middle East, whole villages with the people included were bought and sold like any piece of real estate. The behavior of the masses of the people in this underdeveloped world was governed by ancient taboos, tribal customs, and by social practices which in many lands made it improper for women even to show their faces. The rural population did not live on farms like the American farmer with his automobile and television set, but lived in villages of mud and thatched huts from which they walked out to their little plots in the village fields each day to work, a task that in much of the world was regarded as degrading and only for the lowest classes. Farmers in these countries had never experienced the spirit of independence and self-determination, or the freedom of choice and the ability to act for their own improvement which was fundamental in the experience of the American farmer.

Before the people in the underdeveloped world could be expected to receive and make maximum use of technical and economic aid from the United States they had to become socially, politically, and mentally prepared to receive it. Their government had to establish an administrative system by which they could be reached. They had to acquire a new initiative, a new feeling of confidence in themselves and their government. They had to change certain customs, attitudes of mind, and social institutions that for hundreds, in some cases thousands, of years had stood as mighty barriers to any form of economic progress. Under these circumstances the standard approach of United States agricultural extension, or of any other established method, was not likely to yield notable results. Nor did the large supplies of United States money bring about the changes that were needed.

The people in the peasant villages had to be met where they were, not where a technician with his own set of professional interests and preconceived notions wished them to be. The kind of guidance that was needed was not the job of a technical expert on how to produce more eggs, grow taller corn, or put on demonstrations in soil testing. It was a natural and ready-made job for community development, but the ICA and its predecessor agencies handling America's foreign aid program showed little evidence of knowing anything about the concept of community development. Instead, it was decided to build the foreign aid agency into a departmentalized organization of specialties in line with the standard operating procedures of government bureaucracy. This meant in effect that an assortment of technicians from the various specialized fields were put on the federal payroll to set up an operation around the world that attempted to fit the people and governments of the underdeveloped countries into pre-established professional molds.

Fresh from a culture of the mid-twentieth century in which knowledge had been broken into millions of pieces and carefully arranged into narrow compartments of interest, experts on hybrid corn, sanitation, road building, and other miscellaneous items were sent to the ancient civilizations of the Orient, the Middle East, Africa, and Latin America. Confronted by cultures they did not comprehend, by customs and beliefs they did not fathom, by languages they could not speak, and by people whose thoughts and actions represented one great mystery, these technicians were given the job of causing their systems for increasing the efficiency of agriculture, and of other things, to be put into practice.

The array of specialties, each with its own separate approach disconnected and uncoordinated, was singularly inadequate to cope with the conditions of the underdeveloped world, but these facts did not seem to penetrate to the planners in Washington. And so the corps of technicians were sent out. Tons of films and demonstration materials on how to do it, heavy machinery, and modern farm implements were shipped overseas. Irrigation systems were installed, wells were drilled, swamps were drained, public works were constructed, scientific methods of agriculture were introduced, and glowing reports were sent back to Washington showing impressive lists of results achieved and asking for more money. But in the vastness of Asia, the Middle East, Africa, and Latin America, the results and the money were swallowed up, and the methods did not take. Peasants watched in bewilderment, some ran for cover, and the aged civilizations, impervious to twentieth-century progress by American methods of departmentalized, disciplinary procedure, remained untouched and unmoved in their ancient molds.

The majority of the people in the newly developing countries of the world may be primitive and uneducated, but among the minority who form the upper classes, who make up the national officialdom and occupy the positions of leadership and intellectual attainment both inside and outside government, are some of the most articulate, sophisticated, and highly educated people in the world. Among these people are many who have studied and traveled extensively in Europe and the United States. These people not only know the culture of the West, but thoroughly understand their own cultures and have keen insight into the problems of their countries. An honest fusion of the knowledge of these people with that of the Americans would have been likely to have produced a truly effective program for achieving the goals of foreign aid. But in the underdeveloped world such fusion would have resulted in approaches quite different from those which had been practiced in the United States, and with a few notable exceptions, the attitude of ICA's Washington specialists was always one of being so superior that this fusion was never possible.

The futility of attempting to make a significant difference in the life conditions of newly developing countries by simply transplanting the standard operating procedures of agricultural extension and other specialized fields of professional interest in the United States was soon recognized by many leaders in the countries being aided. Although appreciative of the financial support and the basic good intentions of the Americans, these people knew that the medicine being prescribed by the technicians who had been sent to deliver the aid was not strong enough to do the job. These were societies that were deeply and seriously ill. Recommending improved seed or better methods of livestock breeding was like trying to cure a case of appendicitis with an aspirin tablet. Teachings in literacy, in how to do better farming, how to build latrines, how to provide safe drinking water, and other such technical information were important, but were not enough.

Because the need for a broader approach was recognized by national leaders in many countries, the concept of community development began to spread around the world. The germ of this idea may be traced through many roots into a variety of programs that resulted from the work of many persons operating in different parts of the world with little knowledge of each other. But from the standpoint of its application on a nationwide scale, the primary origin of the idea was in a program started by the British to help prepare colonial people for self-government.

The British first called this work mass education. It grew out of a belief that in the traditional societies of the underdeveloped countries the realization of responsible citizenship must begin at the local level if a solid foundation is to be established for the development of a democratic state, and if economic progress is to be achieved within the framework of a free society. This work of the British was described in a report published in 1944 by an advisory committee to the British secretary of state as a program aimed at "getting people everywhere to be aware of, to understand and take part in, and ultimately to control the economic and social changes which were taking place among them." By the use of educational films, radio broadcasts, posters, and other forms of mass media, the British attempted to teach the people how to organize themselves to make their homes and communities better places in which to live.

The program was planned in such a way as to deal with each village or community, as a whole or "as the unit to be educated," and within this operation all specialized fields of knowledge, such as agriculture and public health, necessary to the improvement of the whole community were introduced in a coordinated effort. The program was carried out in such a way as to encourage the formation of local institutions or organizations through which the people would be better able to manage their own affairs. It was intended as an outside stimulant with the idea that once stimulated the people in each village would go forward on their own initiative.

At a conference held in 1948, the British decided to drop the term "mass education" and to adopt in its place the term "community development," which was defined as "a movement designed to promote better living for the whole community with the active participation, and if possible on the initiative of the community, but if this initiative is not forthcoming spontaneously, by the use of techniques for arousing and stimulating it in order to secure its active and enthusiastic response to the movement." Within a few years this work was extended into more and more villages in the British colonies and gradually began to emerge in the form of national programs in a number of newly independent countries.

The United Nations Secretariat established a special unit called the Community Development Group which sent advisors to help spread the idea in countries all over the world, and began holding international community development conferences. Official statements issued by the United Nations said that community development was made up of two elements: " . . . participation by the people themselves in efforts to improve their level of living with as much reliance as possible on their own initiative," and "the provision of technical and other services in ways which encourage initiative, self-help, and mutual help and make these more effective." Within a few years the idea began to catch the interest of people in many countries, and demands for acceptance and support of community development as an essential approach to the problems of newly developing nations were vigorously registered with ICA missions all over the world.

Under these circumstances it became impossible for the ICA completely to ignore the idea, though recognition and supporting action came slowly and grudgingly. Many of the officials of the principal ICA technical services, particularly agricultural extension, continued to resist the idea as much as possible, some even to the point of open hostility. This opposition was based primarily on a failure to grasp the new concept, and on the fear that it would cut into some of the job positions in their established technical services. The effect of this opposition was illustrated by the difficulties of Raymond H. Rignall in his efforts to support community development in Guatemala even after he had received orders from Washington to stop using the term. Despite this opposition, however, there were some foreign aid officials who saw the potential of community development for providing millions of people with an experience in democracy and thus helping to build their social and economic life. These included such people as Carl Taylor, one of America's leading sociologists, who for many years was an official in the Department of Agriculture, and M. L. Wilson, the father of agricultural extension in the United States.

Important support in Washington came also from certain

members of Congress. As various members of Congress traveled around the world, community development was one of the things that impressed them most favorably. In March 1957, the Senate Foreign Relations Committee, under the chairmanship of Senator Mike Mansfield, issued a report on United States technical assistance programs which said:

The agricultural and community development programs in India deserve a share of the credit for fulfillment of the agricultural goals of the Indian first 5-year plan. The community development program in particular is resulting in changing, more democratic attitudes between villagers and Government officials.

The village aid projects in Pakistan [from which ICA later withdrew its support] and the village development work of the Near East Foundation in Iran (financed in part by ICA funds) are also making significant contributions to the development of these two countries and to the achievement of United States goals. . . . The subcommittee feels that with better planning, examples of this kind can be multiplied and examples of waste can be eliminated. . . . Results of the kind the United States is seeking depend in large measure upon the readiness and willingness of the recipient country to make the most effective use of technical assistance.

In time, the United States foreign aid agency found that the demand for community development was increasing in many of the countries for which aid was intended, and it was necessary to budget certain funds through community development channels; by 1954, growing pressure resulted in the foreign aid agency establishing its small Community Development Division.

Named to head this new division was Louis M. Miniclier, who had represented the State Department in its work with the United Nations in the field of social affairs. Formally trained in social work, he had spent considerable time overseas with the American government, had given much thought to the idea of community development, and was thoroughly convinced that this program was an essential key to successful foreign aid. But despite all Miniclier tried to do personally, the community development approach never received any substantial ICA support. The Community Development Division was so far below the ICA policy-making level that Miniclier was never able to make his voice really count, and in relation to the huge ICA organization of which it was a part, this division was about the size of a broom closet in the Empire State Building. To the major ICA technical services community development opened the door for a new type of approach into which they might become integrated, thus reducing the power and control over programming which their offices enjoyed as separate and independent operations.

Then there were other obstacles. From the academic world came sociologists, anthropologists, and others, each of whom saw community development as just a method of applying principles which they claimed as theirs. Thus, community development found itself squeezed between its enemies representing the traditional technical services within the bureaucracy, and the people outside who ostensibly were its friends representing an assortment of academic disciplines. Its enemies did not want it to exist, and its friends wanted to swallow it up.

Gradually, with the help of a few academic leaders such as Paul S. Taylor at the University of California, Miniclier made some headway toward convincing his academic friends that community development was not just an expression of sociology, or anthropology, or social work, or public administration, but was in fact a new field of effort requiring special skills of its own in which knowledge from many disciplines was brought together with new principles to form a new approach aimed at developing democracy and human freedom around the world.

A further obstacle was created by the fact that in many countries in which programs were carried on under the name of community development, the operations were actually nothing more than an effort to encourage public works projects with peasant labor. This misuse of the term occurred over wide areas of the world, thereby creating added resistance.

In October 1956, after many months of painful struggle

and compromise within its own internal power structure, the ICA came out with an official community development policy statement which was sent to all USOM's overseas. This statement was carefully worded to acknowledge the community development idea, yet still make it possible for the technical services to continue in their own separate ways.

The statement referred to community development as:

a process of social action in which the people of a community organize themselves for planning and action; define their common and individual needs and problems; make group and individual plans to meet their needs and solve their problems; execute these plans with a maximum of reliance upon community resources; and supplement these resources when necessary with services and material from governmental and non-governmental agencies outside the community. . . . Community development fosters a unified approach. . . . It capitalizes and puts to work manpower, the greatest resource of underdeveloped countries. It produces its own end result in the form of experience and skill in democratic procedures. . . .

The ICA statement of community development policy was issued only as general "guidelines," to be used as "may be needed." It was reiterated in 1960, when the director of ICA, in testimony prepared for Congress, cited community development as evidence of imagination in ICA. The issuing of the statement in 1956 and its reiteration in 1960 was a step forward. But it was not very good evidence of imagination in ICA. The concept did not originate in ICA. Few USOM directors and other ICA officials understood its basic meaning as a political force for the building of democratic institutions. As a practical matter the marginal support that community development received, even that which came from members of Congress, was largely smothered under the agricultural extension power structure. The adoption of community development as a part of ICA policy in 1956 was never translated into substantial action at the operating level, and the jealous determination of the major technical services to prevent this broad concept from encroaching any further than necessary into their established empires within the bureaucracy remained solid. Even in the face of continuing demands from the underdeveloped parts of the world, only sixty community development advisors were employed in the entire ICA organization in seventeen out of sixty-four USOM's in 1960. Many of these advisors had no practical experience in community development work and were inhibited by attitudes within their USOM's from doing little more than making studies, writing reports, and holding pleasant academic discussions. By 1960 the Community Development Division in Washington had grown to a total staff of thirteen, counting the typists.

Gradually, many leaders in the underdeveloped world lost hope for any real leadership from the United States in this vital field, and lost confidence in the foreign aid agency's ability to understand their needs. Around the world, leaders in other countries grew to feel that the ICA knew less about community development than they did. An official of the government in Iran told me that in his opinion the only hope for community development in his country was for the ICA to stop interfering with it. In Southeast Asia, a United Nations representative told me, "ICA could give community development enough push to secure freedom in this part of the world and save the American taxpayers a lot of money, but the attitude of your ICA officials is hopeless."

At a United Nations planning conference in Bangkok in December 1960, one of the Asian delegates strongly insisted that the agenda for the 1961 United Nations community development conference include a formal discussion of the problems that were being created by the ICA in countries that were attempting to establish national community development programs. One of the Asian delegates at this Bangkok conference said to me in a personal letter: "The infighting within the ICA organization and the red tape in connection with foreign aid have produced such a disgust that representatives of these countries [in Asia] wanted to compare notes with other nations and specifically take up this problem within the United Nations organization." Actually, there was no justifiable reason for conflict between community development and the operations of agricultural extension, education, public health, and other ICA technical services. Community development could not function successfully without these services and each of them would have produced far greater results within the framework of a community development program than they produced without it.

But while Communist subversion moved through Asia and the Middle East, while the tribes of Africa's new nations grew restless, while revolutionary forces permeated the depressed 90 per cent of Latin America's millions, and the agents of Khrushchev and Mao Tse-tung spread over the globe, policy and routine became pretty well set in the Washington offices of the ICA. Corps of clerks and minor officials went about their daily shuffling of papers, memo and report writing, committee meetings, and coffee breaks. The hungry millions; the disease-ridden, filthy, mud villages; the political stresses and strains of underdeveloped countries; the frantic efforts of the Communists to stir discontent seemed remote and unreal. The planning of strategy by the various offices to enlarge and maintain spheres of bureaucratic influence, to guard against possible encroachment by other sections, to keep higher officials duly impressed, and to handle inquiring congressmen, occupied a healthy percentage of each working day.

In foreign aid missions in capital cities around the world, replicas of this routine were repeated daily, modified by the location and the work at hand. Individually the vast majority of the men and women who made up the system were high-grade Americans willing and anxious to serve their country. But there was some thing odious about the system. Certainly it was not what one might have expected of the "bold new program" to build freedom in a seriously threatened world. Somehow the idealism implicit in foreign aid and in the American dream failed to come through.

In September 1961, new legislation, the Act for International Development, was passed by Congress. In its statement of policy the Act read:

It is the sense of the Congress that peace depends on wider recognition of the dignity and interdependence of men, and survival of free institutions in the United States can best be assured in a worldwide atmosphere of freedom. . . . The Congress declares it to be a primary necessity, opportunity, and responsibility of the United States . . . to help make a historic demonstration that economic growth and political democracy can go hand in hand to the end that an enlarged community of free, stable, and self-reliant countries can reduce world tensions and insecurity. . . .

Soon after the passage of this Act the functions of the ICA were absorbed into the newly created Agency for International Development (AID), and community development was relegated to an even lesser role than it had before. The new foreign aid agency began its operations by making many changes in the old bureaucracy; but until the potential of community development as an instrument for the building of democracy in the emerging countries of the world is given full recognition, the foreign aid program of the United States government will not result in the "historic demonstration" called for in the Act for International Development of 1961. It is the lack of action for the building of viable democratic institutions through which the forces within nations can be united that has thus far resulted in the failure of United States foreign aid to live up to the hopes and intentions of the American people. This is the needed action that national programs of community development, properly carried out, could provide.

4

THE VISION OF INDIA

THE YEAR 1952* MARKED THE BEGINNING OF THE MOST gigantic effort in human history consciously to change the life conditions of a nation by democratic means. This was the official launching by Prime Minister Nehru of India's national program of community development, a calculated plan to energize and give moral impetus to the dormant human resources of a vast sub-continent of 400 million people. It was a plan in which millions of Indian villagers would unite their efforts with those of the government for the physical and social rebuilding of this ancient land. Starting as a pilot project covering 27,388 villages with a population of 16.4 million, this mammoth program now spreading over the country is scheduled by 1963 to cover all of India's nearly 560,000 villages.

It is a moving and dramatic test that may well determine whether or not it is possible for the people of Asia to satisfy their quest for material comforts by invoking the ideals of freedom and human equality, and by so doing gain the richness of that which exists only in the realm of the humane and the spiritual. Perhaps it is a paradox that in this great movement India is striving to preserve the traditions which she cherishes from a civilization of five thousand years

* India's community development program was officially launched on October 2, 1952, the eighty-fourth anniversary of the birth of Mahatma Gandhi.

68

while at the same time advancing into the technological age of the twentieth century.

For the future of the free world it is an experiment that must not fail, for this movement in India is Asia's alternative to the other great Asian experiment now being proclaimed in Communist China. The central issue in both experiments is economic. By one means or another the hundreds of millions who inhabit the vast reaches of Asia are going to share in the economic prosperity of the present age. To attain that end, China has chosen its method. In its program of community development, India has chosen another.

While the leaders of Communist China are attempting to destroy the concept of community, the leaders of India are attempting to build it. In India the concept of community development is linked to the inherent goodness of life itself. It is in the value that, through five millennia, India has come to place upon the village as a unit of society. It is in the Hindu belief in the value of the individual despite the apparent conflicts in its system of caste. It is in the centuries of striving for independence, in the upsurge of nationalism, and in the native pride of India. It is in the spiritual heritage of Gandhi, who, in his long struggle to relate the goal of independence to the needs of the masses and establish in the mind and body of India a human brotherhood, became known as the Mahatma, or the "Great Soul." These are the values that are implicit in India's philosophy of community development.

In the magnificent dream that the Indian community development program represents, there are two distinct and essential aspects to be blended together. A great Indian citizen captured by the spirit of Gandhi expressed it to me in Delhi: "One aspect," he said, "is *community,* and the other is *development."* The aspect of *community* means the cultivation and enrichment of the soul, the spirit, and the feeling of the village as a social body. By this spirit the people are individually and collectively infused with concern for the general welfare. It is a spiritual quality by which the people are inspired to work and act in ways that will contribute to lifting the material standards of village life. It is a spirit that creates not only a village effort, but which instills into that effort a quality of cooperation, responsibility, and interpersonal respect by which the very effort becomes an experience of spiritual beauty that deepens and strengthens human brotherhood within the village. This is the aspect of *community* inherent in the modern dream of India.

Then there is the other aspect—*development*. This aspect of India's program includes the growth of the spiritual, but other qualities are within the intangible boundaries of that spirit as well. *Development* is technology. It is science. It is mechanics and engineering. It is administration. It is capital and natural resources. It is equipment, supplies, and materials. This is *development*. It is the combination of both these aspects—*community* and *development*—that will enable the program in India to succeed.

Thus the spirit of community must exist within the villages, and where it does not exist it must be created. Embraced within that spirit must be the qualities of eagerness, recognition of need, organization for intelligent village planning and action, and willingness to receive and use whatever outside aid may be needed. Simultaneously with the creation and activation of that spirit, and fused into the process of creating it, adequate delivery must be made of technical knowledge, of capital and credit, and of materials and equipment. When the spirit of community and the ingredients of development such as proper seed, fertilizer, irrigation, tools and technical knowledge are synthesized within the village, the goals set forth in India's five-year plans will be attained with relative ease and without damage to the cultural qualities which India wishes to preserve.

But India is a vast country of contrasts and contradictions, of elations and disappointments. Within her borders are the elements of hope and promise for the realization of her dream. Yet the gap between vision and reality is enormous; for also inside her borders are powerful obstructions—ugly, narrow, cruel, indolent qualities—that threaten to crush and defeat the great experiment upon which she has embarked.

I had long read and heard of the contrasts of the subcontinent and upon arrival in Delhi in 1960 aboard Air India began immediately to encounter them. I checked in at the Ashoka, one of the most fashionable hotels in all Asia, visited with members of the elite in exquisite buildings, and drove through streets lined by lush flowers and trees and palatial homes. From Delhi to Calcutta to Bombay, I sampled the splendors of India, eloquent testimony to a great civilization that used to be and of what could be in the future. I experienced the wonders of the Taj Mahal at Agra, the enchantment of Darjeeling and the Himalayas, and felt the spell of the vast works of Hindu art.

But the sheer magnitude of human need was overwhelming. Four hundred million human beings multiplying by as many as there are in New York City every year, with nearly six times as many people per square mile as there are in the United States was a number that could only seep into my brain as I moved through the country and experienced the endless swarm of humanity. Everywhere, along dusty country roads, in mud-walled, ancient villages, and in crowded city streets there were always people—people standing, sitting, lying down, or moving.

In the cities was the seemingly endless labyrinth of passageways—alleys and narrow streets lined on either side by multi-storied buildings with sheets of dirty cloth and ragged clothes hanging from upper windows, a veritable clutter of brightly colored signs in English, Hindi, and other languages, and rows of narrow openings into shops in which men squatted along the walls selling their wares. On the sidewalks there were crowds of street vendors with merchandise ranging from dime-store trinkets to spoiling food spread out on pieces of cloth exposed to the flies and the dirt from human, animal, and vehicular traffic. Here and there was a Hindu shrine, and next to one of them a large Mobilgas sign with its flying red horse.

Filling the sidewalks and overflowing into the center

stream of movement, masses of brown-skinned people mingled with two-wheeled carts, swarms of bicycles, horse-drawn buggies, tricycle taxis, automobiles, stray cattle, and dogs. Underfoot was the thick flattened mush of accumulated animal waste, garbage, refuse, and miscellaneous dirt, and overhead a maze of telephone and electric wires to add to the mixture of the modern with the ancient. Wet with sweat from the heat and humidity, I wormed my way along the streets, shielded my eyes from the sun, and breathed the putrid odors of decaying organic matter that seemed to saturate the air.

The mass of people in motion in white flowing garments punctuated by the bright blues, reds, greens, golds, and other colors of the crowd gave sharp accent to the panorama of the Orient. There were bejewelled women with smooth, jet-black hair hanging in braids to their waists over bright-colored *saris,* and there were others clad in rags. There were men in *dhotis*. Others wore pieces of multi-colored material wrapped skirt-like around their waists, and in Calcutta a man walked unnoticed along the street with nothing on at all. There were Sikhs in turbans, and people in Western clothes. In crowded streets I watched naked children splashing, wading, and urinating in open water tanks where women washed clothes and others stood in line to draw water from a rickety pump and to fill brass and earthen containers for household use.

In rancid, crowded flats above the street level I visited places where as many as a dozen lived in a single room. The stairways and hallways provided space for emaciated people, half alive, though with enough strength remaining to reach out for alms. There were seemingly endless blocks of rat-infested buildings such as these. Then there were the slums, the unending rows of make-shift shacks thrown up from pieces of tin, cardboard, and sticks amid seas of filth and junk piled halfway up the walls, with ceilings too low to permit standing. How many thousands inhabit these shacks God only knows; then there were the others, the herds of human wrecks who live and die in the streets.

But the cities and towns represent only about 20 per cent of the people of India. The other 80 per cent live in villages where poverty and ignorance are more uniformly spread than in the cities.

No one knows the exact age of most Indian villages, though they are commonly several hundred, some more than a thousand, years old. Each village is a distinct unit of territory situated in the open country, consisting of crude huts and buildings and an area of land for agriculture. The character of the villages varies greatly from one part of the country to another, but virtually all of them are primitive, dirty, and poor. Many of them are connected to the outside world only by dirt roads that wash out during the monsoons and become almost invisible in the dust of dry weather. The lack of drainage makes most of the villages quagmires when it rains, and the absence of plumbing or of even outdoor toilets, along with the clutter of pigs, chickens, and cows, and a habit of the housewives of throwing refuse into the streets, results in a medium for the spread of disease that would kill many Westerners accustomed to modern sanitation. People commonly go into the fields to eliminate, though it is not uncommon to see children and even adults defecating along the side of a village street.

The houses may be clustered into a compact area amid the surrounding fields, inside which narrow passageways zigzag among the houses, forming openings almost like tunnels without roofs. These passageways, and frequently the houses on either side, are shared by humans and animals alike. The streets are swept by the lowest members of the village called sweepers, and powdered cow dung mixed in water is sometimes sprinkled over the surface. In better villages the streets are kept relatively clean, and in some there are even paved streets and sidewalks. Many of the villages are quite open with ample space, sometimes even fields, between the houses, but there is always a well-established area of land identified with each village. These ancient pockets of human settlement, bound tightly unto themselves in culture and tradition, and ranging in population from a hun-

dred or so people to a few thousand are dotted over the
length and breadth of the sub-continent.

Beginning some four thousand years ago with the Aryan
invasion of India from central Asia, the rigid social division
known as caste gradually spread over the land and became
established as a way of life. Today, conditions are gradually
changing, but village India is still divided internally by caste,
and by family groups. Within the villages people are deeply
influenced by ancient prejudices and superstitions including
beliefs in black magic, and by an ingrained conservatism
against the introduction of new ideas. Many diseases and
village problems are felt to be the will of the gods or of dis-
pleased ancestral ghosts. Fertilizer is believed by many to
poison the soil, and most Indian farmers can still be seen
cultivating the fields with primitive wooden plows drawn by
bullocks, many of whom are too weak from undernourish-
ment to pull a normal load. Over large areas of the country,
I watched villagers spreading cow dung in rows for drying
in the sun, after which it is neatly placed in round, even
stacks to be used as fuel, thus further depleting the already
tired and worn-out soil. In the country as a whole the vast
majority of the population is illiterate, but in many of the
villages illiteracy is almost complete. Ignorance, indolence,
and an almost unbelievably low productivity blanket the
country. I saw roads being constructed by women carrying
pans of gravel on their heads. Nationwide, the average per
capita income is less than $1.25 a week, and it has been
estimated that at present rates of increase it will take until
1986 to lift the weekly per capita earnings to an even $2.
No matter what advances are made, whether in the construction of schools or in increased agricultural productivity,
the lag between achievements attained and the ever-rising
population is always present.

In the face of these and a myriad of allied problems demanding attention, India is in many respects not truly one,
but many. Added to the ancient disunity created by caste, by
sectional differences among geographical regions, and by the
isolation of village populations, deep fissures have resulted

from bitter religious strife. Now other divisive forces have arisen in the form of widespread agitation for a division of states on the basis of language. In addition to Hindi and English, the Indian constitution recognizes thirteen official languages, and more than eight hundred dialects are spoken in the various parts of the country. Already fifteen states have been organized largely along language barriers, and further divisions are being sought.

In this kind of a setting the government of India has attempted to master the vast problems of logistics and co-ordination of forces that are essential to a successful national program of community development.

Long before the official launching of the program in 1952, numerous village improvement efforts had been started both by Indians and foreigners. Many of these efforts were the work of missionaries. In Madras a great deal of work aimed at improving villages had been sponsored by the YMCA. Another project was started by a British citizen near Delhi. Experiments in village development were engaged in by Tagore whose writings, including the Indian national anthem, exerted profound influence upon the life of India. Other such experiments were conducted by Gandhi himself.

In 1948, a pilot project in village development was started in the state of Uttar Pradesh with the assistance of Albert Mayer, an American architect and planner who went to India in 1942 as an officer of the United States Army Engineers. Mayer developed a deep interest in the country and became personally acquainted with Jawaharlal Nehru shortly after the future prime minister was released from a British jail where he had been confined for his activities in the move for Indian independence. Later Mayer returned to India in private capacity and under the sponsorship of the Uttar Pradesh government helped plan and carry out the pilot project. This project began in sixty-four villages and was extended within three years to more than three hundred villages in the district of Etawah. It was also carried out in four other areas of the state. This work of Albert Mayer and his associates, with the personal encouragement of

Nehru, became an early working model for the mammoth community development program which the government of India was eventually to extend throughout the nation.

As the government program has evolved, it has been designed to focus attention on a number of specific goals that have been determined by government planners as national targets in the Indian five-year plans. These are goals which can be accomplished only if the great mass of people who live in the villages can be persuaded to adopt attitudes, practices, habits, customs, and desires that are favorable to their attainment, and can at the same time be encouraged to go to work for them. Thus, a basic change must be made in centuries of established tradition, the whole outlook of village India reoriented, and hundreds of millions of agrarian people mobilized in an intelligent, unified effort, village by village, throughout the country.

The first of the national goals is food production. Agriculture is the mainstay of village India. Seventy per cent or more of the nation's total population depends upon it for a livelihood, yet production has never been high enough to provide for India's teeming millions. The community development program continually urges special projects to induce the villagers to adopt improved methods of cultivation, plant high quality seed, use proper fertilizers and manures, and accept other practices that will build up the fertility of the land.

Projects in the construction and use of irrigation systems, better animal breeding and grazing practices, the planting of trees, the use of better implements, and scores of other techniques of modern farming are introduced in the villages and continuously urged upon the people.

The organization of cooperatives of all kinds is a major effort to help solve the problem of land holdings that are too small to make economic farm units, expand grossly inadequate rural credit, build up the formation of capital, and add to the powers of the masses in marketing, production, and consumption—not only in agriculture, but in other fields of activity such as small-scale industries.

A third goal is the development of small-scale industries. This includes cottage industries, or the hand manufacture of items by people in their homes. It includes the development of small village manufacturing centers to process agricultural products and other materials for local use, and the establishment of small plants that may be able to compete successfully with large-scale industry. This project is aimed at creating new job opportunities for the millions of people in rural India who are either unemployed or are engaged in agricultural pursuits but are unable to make a living because they are idle most of the year.

A fourth area of emphasis is the construction and maintenance by the villagers of an improved network of rural roads. It is felt that this goal is necessary to make possible a more efficient movement of goods, and to open the flow of new ideas that will stimulate modern thinking, thus hastening the breakdown of rigid patterns in Indian society which today stand as ancient barriers to national progress.

A fifth goal is health and sanitation. This includes the establishment of village dispensaries and clinics, the use of modern medicine, services for maternity and the care of children, and education in family planning. It includes the promotion of good health habits such as medical examinations and proper nutrition, the control of communicable diseases, school health programs, the development of sewage disposal, latrines, drainage, safe drinking water, and other sanitary facilities, and the promotion of clean, hygienic overall living conditions within the villages.

A sixth area of emphasis for the community development program is the rebuilding of village housing in order to provide clean, satisfactory living quarters for each family.

A seventh goal is social welfare. This is closely related to some of the other goals of the program, and includes such items as the care and rehabilitation of the handicapped, and the development of voluntary social services and of activities for children and adults that will promote the general welfare.

Another goal is what the government refers to as education and social education: the development of adequate schools to help implement a section in the national constitution that provides free, compulsory education for all Indian children through fourteen years of age. It also means the establishment of adult education programs including literacy training. But it means much more than that. The central purpose of this part of the program is, to use the government's own words, "to impart to the rural people community sense, corporate outlook, and social consciousness." Toward this end the villagers are urged to organize and maintain community centers for a wide variety of village activities both educational and recreational, to establish women's organizations, youth clubs, and other types of groups that will help encourage greater village spirit and increase the community's ability to engage in an organized effort for its own improvement. The community development program also promotes the establishment of elected *panchayats,* or village councils, which have been provided for in the laws of the various Indian states, and helps carry out a national policy to which India now refers as democratic decentralization.

The major over-all goal is to develop within the minds of more than 300 million rural people an attitude, a sense of social responsibility, and a desire for an organized citizens' effort that will inspire, stimulate, and enable this vast reservoir of Indian manpower to join forces with the government in a great countrywide effort to uplift the quality of life in nearly 560,000 villages, thereby laying the foundation for the social, economic, and political advancement of all India.

One of the fundamental principles in the underlying philosophy of the Indian approach is that the community development program should not be superimposed from above, but should be an expression of the will of the people, with the government in the role of a guide and helper. It must be geared to the minds of the villagers. Only in this way, says the government, can the program have an enduring effect and bring about the desired change in the basic nature of

In the rugged Krikellon area of rural Greece the author watches a housewife bake bread in a special type oven designed for village homes in the area. High quality grain and improved family nutrition have become important parts of the Krikellon community development program. (*CARE*)

George D. Taylor, chief of CARE's Korean Mission, offers prayer to the Sea God for good catch, safe return of fisherman at food ceremony in Nam Hae prior to launching of new fishing boats built from materials contributed by the American people through CARE. With civic organization inspired by Taylor, the people in many Korean communities are working together to raise their standard of living. (*CARE*)

With steel tracks and cars supplied through CARE, Korean villagers work together to build salt works along the Yellow Sea, using ancient foot pumps to get water from the sea. They will let the salt settle, sell it to help build their local economy. Many people are beginning to learn that by working together in a system of democratic organization they can make new progress toward a better life.

In Philippine *barrio* (village), residents gather for news and educational broadcasts by a radio supplied through CARE. The *barrio* people will use what they hear as springboard for discussions in their community development meeting. (*CARE*)

Agricultural improvements—a vital part of community development throughout the world. In the Philippines, it has been learned that improvements in agriculture can be stimulated within the framework of a community development program much more readily than is possible outside such a program. (*CARE*)

Harold Sillcox, CARE mission chief to Vietnam, who helped lead the development of "Lucky Village," (*left foreground*) attends presentation of decorticating machine—a machine that will travel from village to village, breaking banana stalks into fiber, which the people can then process into twine for woven sacks used to ship rice and other grains. (*CARE*)

Señora Elisa Molina de Stahl ("Moli") on one of her many visits to help the depressed people of rural Guatemala.

A group of Indian farmers examines the newly arrived CARE hand tool package containing a spading fork, weeding hoe, rake, and shovel. These modern tools, being provided to thousands of small farmers in India, are part of the community development program through which CARE is helping them to raise farm production and thus the standard of living.

(*CARE*)

the country. Thus, it becomes, according to the philosophy behind it, a program of aided self-help, with the government supplying the aid and the villagers the self-help.

A further principle in this Indian approach is that all of the various government services required by the villagers to achieve the goals of the program should be delivered in a coordinated and integrated way, instead of separately and individually with each government department acting unilaterally. This principle considers the community not as a system of separate and isolated functions such as agriculture, health, education, unrelated to each other, but as a unit of society in which all of these functions exist as interrelated parts of the community as a whole. It is a philosophy which recognizes the fact that the solution of any one community problem is dependent upon the solution of many other problems, and that because the community is in itself a web of human interactions and interrelationships, the basic unit of concern in community development must be the community itself. Thus, it is within this framework of a program directed at the community that the government's specialized services in agriculture and other fields are to be delivered.

To carry out this comprehensive program, the government has built up a huge and complex bureaucracy beginning with a Ministry of Community Development to provide coordination at the national level, and reaching out through ever descending lines of authority to encompass the entire country. General policy and over-all planning and direction are centered in the national capital at New Delhi, but responsibility for the actual operations of the program is vested in the state governments.

A central committee at the top is concerned with broad policy. It includes members from the Ministries of Community Development and Food and Agriculture, and the National Planning Commission, with the prime minister serving as chairman. This committee is assisted by an advisory board consisting of representatives of a number of other ministries. In each state there is a development committee chaired by the chief minister of the state, with a commissioner of development serving in a coordinating and administrative capacity at the state level similar to that of the minister of community development at the national level. The Indian states are divided into districts, each with a district development committee chaired by the collector who is the chief government officer at that level, and whose personal influence makes him one of the most important executives in the entire program.

The jurisdictional areas of the district collectors are divided into development blocks which constitute the basic units of administration in the field. Each block covers an average of about 150 to 170 square miles in which there are approximately 100 villages with some 60,000 to 70,000 people. The current practice is to schedule the development blocks for two stages of operation of five years each, with the intensity of government service being reduced in the second stage. A standard block budget of twelve lakhs of rupees (about $240,000) is allocated for operations during the first stage, and five lakhs (about $100,000) for the second.

Plans call for a field operating staff of technicians covering each of the specified goals of the program—agriculture, cooperatives, small-scale industry, social education, etc.,—to be assigned to each block. These technicians receive technical supervision from their parent agencies, but are responsible for purposes of coordination and administration to a block development officer who works under the supervision of the district collector. In addition to these specialists who are to serve all the villages in the development block, there is a crew of employees for each block known as village level workers, or *gram sevaks,* who live in the villages and form the major direct link between the government and the people.

Nehru has often said that the community development program is the most important thing being done in India, and it is. Strong, self-reliant communities competent to deal intelligently with their problems, able to contribute positively to the life of the nation, and to provide their people with lasting values of human and spiritual content are essential to the welfare of modern India. They are fundamental to the development of freedom and a dynamic economy in Asia. The gigantic move in India to create such communities represents the hope not only of India, but of the world. Nehru himself reflects this mood when he says, "The community projects are the bright, vital, and dynamic sparks from which radiate rays of energy, hope, and enthusiasm."

Potentially these rays of energy and hope are present in community development blocks throughout India, but today they are not burning as brightly as they should. Somewhere in the mechanics of the operation the sparks are missing. Somewhere in the inner recesses of the bureaucracy, it has been forgotten that the basic power of the heritage from which the sparks for this movement were generated was not mechanical or technical or administrative, but spiritual. The Great Soul of Gandhi, which is implicit in the philosophy of this program, is embodied not in the characteristics of a government agency, but in the characteristics of love. This is the power that is first essential to the living spirit of community and without that spirit the community development program becomes a lifeless, non-productive effort.

In striving to build the spirit of community and to place in its hands the tools of technology by which the villages of India can move into the future, a system of government procedures has been erected in which the very spirit itself cannot breathe. Here in the most colossal effort in human history to combine spiritual and technological forces for the advancement of man is an organization which has placed emphasis on mustering the forces that are material and technological, but which in practice has given little emphasis to the forces that are spiritual.

In a number of critical ways the program in India has been allowed to violate the basic philosophy of community development to which India is committed. In principle, a bureaucracy has been created to deal with the community as a living whole, and within that framework to deliver in an integrated manner all of the material and technical aids that may be needed by the villagers to achieve increased food production and other national goals. But in practice a collection of splinter projects is being pushed at the villagers, each project being carried on independently and in isolation from the others.

Each specialist at block headquarters has his own project activities to promote, with the block development officer functioning as a government administrative officer but not as an imaginative leader of a community development team. Many block development officers are not community developers either by inclination or by training and experience, and the specialists are too concerned with their own specialties to see the community as a whole.

To a significant extent the community development machinery has become just another bureaucracy. Within its structure there is an assortment of branch departments, one for each of the goals of the program, each operating within the narrow limits of its own specialty as though it were a separate agency only vaguely aware of the concept of community development. Thus, to the normal competition among already existing government agencies has been added the competition of the community development agency within which an unintended tug of war is going on among the specialized branches representing its various goals.

In building the community development bureaucracy, large numbers of persons were drawn into the program who had given no previous thought to community development, but who had been officials and employees in the existing public service which had been designed to enforce laws, collect taxes, and perform other old-line functions of government.

Community development training centers have been established, but the major emphasis in training is on agriculture and other standard specialties, not on the concept and techniques of community development. This means that at the operating level which comes into direct touch with the villagers there is a dearth of personnel with a clear conception of the basic meaning of community development, or of what is necessary to inspire and organize the kind of sustained community effort that will produce the changed attitudes and outlook that must be present if India is to achieve her national goals within the framework of a democratic society. Without these intangible qualities no amount of seed, fertilizer, credit, and technical assistance will enable India to meet the needs of her people by democratic means.

Many technical advisors have recommended that still greater emphasis be placed upon technical knowledge, particularly in the field of agriculture. Certainly, there can be no question of the urgency to increase the production of Indian agriculture or of the need for competent technical assistance in the standard specialties, but this advice ignores the fact that increased agricultural production, as well as other economic goals, will be more likely achieved by Indian villagers within the framework of true community development than will be possible outside that framework.

The critical weakness of the community development program in India is that in actual practice it is in many respects not really community development. Some of the crucial elements in community development that are most lacking in the Indian program are those intangible qualities which are needed to gather the people of the village, lift their sights to the future, infuse into them a sense of initiative, determination, and independence, and set them moving intelligently and confidently with whatever technical and material aid may be needed toward the building of a greater and more prosperous future. Technical and material aids are merely the tools by which India's villagers will build the future, once they have the spirit to use them.

One of the powerful forces within the bureaucracy is an almost overwhelming desire for status, an inner urge to become one of the civil service elite, and to experience the pleasure of issuing orders. This tendency, along with an atmosphere of formality, stiffness, rigidity, and extreme consciousness of levels of authority has become a malignant growth in the community development agency which so influences official behavior that one has to probe to discover the spirit of community. The sweep of officialdom over the country is such that the efforts of private groups, many of which are fully inspired by the drive that India so desperately needs, tend to be looked upon as unwanted competitors meddling in official business, instead of being encouraged and helped to make the contribution of which they are capable.

These official traits, added to the ponderous effort involved in procedures of coordination, and the multiple divisions in job responsibility and specialization of functions, have made it impossible even to synchronize the material aspects of the program. Seed is frequently delivered at the wrong season of the year, fertilizer goes to one village, irrigation to another, a plow to another, and credit is not made ready when it is needed.

When all of these difficulties within the bureaucracy itself are viewed against the extreme difficulty of moving to sustained action hundreds of thousands of ancient, illiterate, poverty-stricken, custom-bound Indian villages even under the most favorable of circumstances, the magnitude of the struggle for progress that is now under way in India becomes clear.

At the bottom of the bureaucratic monster is the last man on the totem pole, the village-level worker. Selected from young men who have lived or had experience in rural areas, and who have a ninth- or tenth-grade education, the village worker is given eighteen months' training in agriculture and six months' training in a variety of other subjects, including something about the theory and practice of community development. He is intended to function as a multi-purpose worker. Having been trained in many practical skills, he is able to teach the villagers many things that would otherwise absorb the time and energies of the more advanced technicians. Thus, the services of the technicians can be more widely spread and more efficiently utilized.

Administratively, the village worker operates under the supervision of the block development officer. For technical supervision he is under the various specialists who have been assigned to the block headquarters. Each village worker is assigned to work in a circle of ten villages within the development block. He lives in one of these villages and travels among the others. He is given the responsibility of acting as a friend, guide, and philosopher to the villagers in these ten villages, and of organizing community effort in all of the fields of activity included in the national community development policy. Working through the village council, he is expected to stimulate the villagers to become aware of their problems, express the needs they feel, plan and take action, teach them the practical knowledge he has been taught, and help them to make full use of the technical advice of the specialists who work out of the block office.

Basically, the idea of the village-level worker is sound, and in a country where surplus manpower is great, and funds and advanced technicians are short, it is probably the only way that technical information of a relatively simple nature can be adequately supplied.

In practice the system has shown weaknesses, due partly to the urge of the technicians for status and authority and to the lack of emphasis in training at all levels on those aspects of community development that are spiritual and organizational in nature, or which constitute community. Closely associated with this problem is the general attitude which has been directed toward the village worker from other members of the community development staff.

According to the government publications, he is the most vital element in the whole system; in practice he is the tiniest, most insignificant, least influential, and most over-worked member of the organization. He is continuously being ordered to do various chores ranging from the castration of scrub bulls to the building of parks for children.

With no one to boss except the villagers, the village worker finds himself between two sets of forces. On the one side are his many bosses; on the other side are the villagers whose traditional emphasis upon the wisdom of age frequently makes them not too receptive to following orders the village worker is charged with getting them to carry out.

In accordance with the philosophy of community development to which India is committed, the village worker has what is perhaps the most difficult job, calling for the greatest personal skill and leadership in the entire program. His is the job of lifting, stimulating, organizing, and teaching the people to release within themselves and their village the vast powers of democratic action. His is the day-to-day job of helping the village to mold itself into a competent human organization, able to understand its basic problems and intelligently make use of the technical and material aids that are available. His is the job of cultivating and nurturing the spiritual incentive that can make progress possible. He is the one who must guide the people to know and feel the spirit of community with all its delicate shades of meanings and overtones, develop their own powers of leadership, and with the incentive that comes from that spirit and leadership build and preserve the inherent greatness of India.

It is a large order for a young man who is supervised by eight or nine officials and technicians who themselves are not community developers and who understand only in the most nebulous way what is required to fill the order.

Since the community development program was started in 1952 the village people have built with government aid many thousands of miles of roads, reclaimed and brought under irrigation millions of acres of land and raised the level of agricultural production. They have built thousands of new schools, community centers, health and sanitary facilities, formed thousands of cooperative societies, and made innumerable other improvements. The complete list of physical achievements is indeed a dramatic story of action involving millions of rural people. No program of this kind has received more favorable publicity or more worldwide attention.

But the fundamental greatness of the movement still lies in its philosophy and its potential for social change and human equality by which the way to progress can be opened. For with all of the physical improvements that could be cited, the work thus far has made little more than an almost imperceptible dent in the human suffering, the grinding poverty, the universal ignorance, the ancient attitudes of a civilization of the past, and the over-all primitive conditions of village life. As yet it cannot be said that village India has awakened to the great vision of its national leaders.

Many educated Indians and leaders outside government say the program has failed. Even the government's own evaluation report issued in July 1960 states:

People's reactions in most of the blocks studied are not yet generally favourable to the growth of self-reliance in village communities which is the primary aim of the C. D. [community development] programme. The majority of the villagers do not regard it as their own and seem to rely mainly on the government for effecting the development of the rural areas. The basic philosophy and approach of the C. D. programme are, therefore, inadequately subscribed to by the people in these areas.

But with all its failings to live up to the greatness of its heritage and its philosophy, the community development program in India is not a failure. Perhaps it has been spread too thin on limited resources, as many people allege. Perhaps it has attempted more than it can manage. Its basic weakness has been in placing emphasis on physical improvements as goals in themselves, instead of means by which a powerful community effort can be built. But it has been an effort to instill democracy into a vast sub-continent where for five millennia there has been no democracy, and it has paved the way for this basic reform.

The reform which India calls democratic decentralization is now in the process of being carried out. Elected village councils carrying legal status, the fundamental units of self-government, have been established throughout the country. These councils, including even women and people who were once untouchables, elect representatives to form block development boards, from which representatives are elected to district boards. These representative boards are to function with independent legal authority in coordinating the community development work and in the setting of policy, with the government staff acting as a secretariat to the people's board in the development blocks. This change represents one of the most profound social changes toward the development of democracy now going on anywhere in the world. It means that a chain of relationships will flow upward from village to block to district, and on up to state and national levels, a direct reversal of the past.

Most important of all, community development has given India new hope for the realization of her dream which has inspired the entire free world. There are evils in the bureaucracy primarily because they have been absorbed from the larger bureaucracy of which the community development agency is a part. When the gap between community development philosophy and practice is closed, which many Indians are striving to do, the government of the second largest population in the world will achieve the unique status of a genuine working partnership with its people in the most gigantic enterprise in human history for building the social and economic welfare of man upon the foundations of a democratic society.

Against the overwhelming problems India has had to face with hopelessly inadequate financial resources, and without adequately trained personnel, it is amazing that the community development program has made as much progress as it has. There is no national program of this kind in the world in which government leaders have been more objective and more openly critical of their own efforts in their determination to increase their effectiveness. Not all the improvements that are needed in the operation can be expected to come quickly, regardless of how much they may be desired by the nation's leaders inside or outside the government. The magnitude of India's problems and the inherent difficulties of forming a new kind of philosophy in any bureaucracy are too great. But for the future of India there is no substitute for the community development program if human freedom is to survive and grow.

One of the dangers is that the desire for spectacular physical results may create a tendency to give up the whole idea and resort to more hasty methods. With technical and financial aid from other countries the government may build great hydro-electric dams, steam generators, heavy industry, highways, vast irrigation systems, and capital formations, which it is already doing and which it must continue. But without the efforts of the great mass of the people to improve themselves and their villages, which community development will ultimately bring if properly applied, these material achievements can never make the changes that are needed in village India. Community development is the only route by which the people of India may eventually gain the knowledge, the feeling, the practice, and the experience they must have to make freedom a living reality, while at the same time building an economy in which they may share in the benefits of the twentieth century.

Community development in India has become a powerful indigenous movement. It has grown from the great surge of independence and the heritage of Gandhi. It has had the leadership of Nehru. Several leading Americans who were in India during its early stages gave it their personal support, including such leaders as Horace Holmes who brought experience in agricultural extension but with an open and imaginative mind; Paul Hoffman, then president of the Ford Foundation which has invested some $11 million in the work; and Chester Bowles, then America's ambassador to India, who personally helped launch the program.

The ICA showed little enthusiasm for the community development idea, and in 1959 withdrew its support from the program, which it had been in the process of doing for the previous two years, even though millions of dollars of United States aid continued to flow into the country. But on the basis of what I learned in New Delhi and in Washington, it is evident that India regarded ICA's advice of little help and was quite willing for it to be withdrawn.

The human qualities that are required to make the program work are by no means lacking in India. These qualities are reflected not only in the program itself but in smaller works such as in Literacy Village near Lucknow which is taking elementary education to India's rural people with aid from CARE and the Ford Foundation. Welthy Fisher, the widow of a Methodist missionary who has devoted many years in India, and who started Literacy Village told me, "In contrast to Communist China which boasts of its great leap forward, India has chosen democracy, and slowly but surely she is making it work."

I saw the truth of Welthy Fisher's words in Indian villages where the community development program has taken hold. I heard it spoken by a great Indian leader who has helped hundreds of families of refugees near Calcutta to build the New Barrackpore Cooperative, and with it a new community and a new life. I saw it in Sheroo Motivala, a dedicated Indian woman who is carrying new hope and determination to villages in the Bombay area as she goes about her work with CARE, and I heard it from a wealthy businessman in his home at Poona. I saw it in the dedication of T. S. Krishnan in the CARE office in Delhi. I saw it in the great works of Lakshma Jain, leader of the Indian Co-operative Union whose life was caught up in the spell of Gandhi. I felt it in the presence of Tarlok Singh, deputy secretary of the National Planning Commission, one of India's great thinkers. And late one day after returning from a village where the people had demonstrated the potential of India's community development program for the building of a new will to advance, a young official in the Ministry of Community Development said this to me: "India's program has had many problems to overcome, and still has. But it will succeed because it must succeed. We are correcting our mistakes. And we have the courage that was left by Gandhi."

"What was Gandhi?" I asked.

"How can I say, what was Gandhi?" he replied. "He gave us faith to live by. He was the commander, the teacher, the leader, the preacher, the friend. How can I say what he was? Gandhi was India."

When this civil servant explained what community development meant to him it was something that gave the mixture that I know India and the whole free world is seeking—a proper mixture of *community* and *development*. In India the possibility of achieving that mixture is being tested. It is not material alone, and it is not spiritual alone. It is a creative synthesis of both. If the vast problems of logistics, administration, training, and organization can be solved, if the skills of stimulation and motivation can be developed, that synthesis will be made, and India will demonstrate to the world the power of democracy and human freedom. Meanwhile, all Asia watches. For as this great test unfolds, the other test is also unfolding in Communist China.

5

THE FIGHTING COCK

STRETCHING OVER MORE THAN FIFTEEN HUNDRED MILES between the South China Sea and the Pacific Ocean are the more than seven thousand islands which in 1946 were granted independence from the United States to become the Republic of the Philippines. In this tropical archipelago with its high mountains rising out of thick jungle plains are an estimated 27.5 million people who comprise one of the exploding populations of Southeast Asia.

In the late 1940's, shortly after the republic had been established, a deep-seated agrarian unrest which had been building up for generations erupted in the form of a Communist-inspired rebellion. For six years this rebellion, led by an army of guerrillas estimated at twenty thousand men known as the Huks, posed a powerful threat to the newly independent government. After bitter fighting the Filipino army succeeded in crushing the main Huk force, though a nagging resistance continued until 1954.

The reasons for the widespread unrest which made this rebellion possible were many and varied, but always came back to the deplorable conditions under which the mass of the people had for so long existed. The great majority of Filipinos lived in villages called *barrios*. For generations the pattern of life had been the same endless toil with little more than life itself to show for the effort. Each morning men, women, and children went out from the *barrios* to work in the fields and rice paddies which to this day make up most of the land that has been opened to farming—less than one-third of the total land area. Millions lived from childhood to death in crowded bamboo-thatched huts built on stilts to help provide ventilation and protect them from dampness and other hazards on the ground. All their lives they had cooked on open stone fireplaces, eaten near-starvation diets of a little rice, a little fish, and a little corn. In the *barrios* there were no sanitary facilities, no safe drinking water, no electricity, no doctors, no privacy. Many of the *barrios* were remote from the more civilized parts of the country, and most of them were not connected by roads. During much of the year, rains made most of the few existing roads impassable. Travel was largely by foot, bullock cart, or boat. Suffering had persisted for so long that sickness and ill-feeling had become normal. The Filipino farmer did not really have a chance, and he had no reason to hope for anything better. For generations the government had paid virtually no attention to the *barrios,* and there were no established organizations through which the people could make any substantial improvement for themselves.

As the state of unrest continued to be expressed in peasant uprisings climaxed by the Huk rebellion, and as communism continued to spread over the Asian mainland, it became increasingly evident that the Philippines was in need of a national program of community development through which hope and stability could be created by bringing the people and government together in a nationwide, organized effort to achieve peaceful and progressive change. Powerful obstacles lay in the path of establishing such a program, but because there were leaders in the Philippines who recognized what was needed and were willing to devote themselves to overcoming the obstacles, this island republic has become the scene of one of the most effective national community development programs created anywhere in the world.

In response to flagrant and widespread election frauds which occurred in 1949, one of the most important voluntary organizations in recent Philippine history was founded—the

National Movement for Free Elections, commonly known as NAMFREL. This organization set out to teach people throughout the islands the importance of honest elections and how to evaluate issues and candidates; but it recognized that election violence and the buying and selling of votes were merely symptomatic of the whole complex of unwholesome conditions that existed in the nation's communities, and that what was therefore needed was a full-scale nationwide community development program.

To help bring such a program into being, twenty-three national organizations were brought together and plans were made for a chain of community centers to be operated by citizens' committees, and to serve as meeting places for as many people as they could get to come in from the surrounding *barrios* to formulate plans for action aimed at community improvement. Each center was to be fully equipped for a program of citizen education in a wide range of practical subjects that would help the people build strength into the body politic.

NAMFREL was headed by a young Filipino army colonel, Jamie N. Ferrer, who had achieved fame as a guerrilla fighter and who was then national commander of the Philippine Veterans Legion. Along with Ferrer, and one of the main sparks behind the NAMFREL campaign, was an idealistic but toughminded ex-colonel of the United States Army, Gabriel L. Kaplan, who had been awarded the Legion of Merit while fighting for the liberation of the Philippines during World War II. Kaplan was a skilled organizer of civic action from New York City, an attorney by profession. Under a grant from the Catherwood Foundation of Bryn Mawr, Pennsylvania, and later with support from a group of prominent American citizens operating as the Committee for Philippine Action in Development, Reconstruction, and Education, Kaplan served as NAMFREL's counselor and was instrumental in obtaining the backing of CARE. CARE, which had already opened a mission in Manila, accepted the challenge of raising funds to equip the NAMFREL community centers with tools, machinery, and other self-help equipment.

There were many factors which led to the establishment of the national community development program in the Philippines. But it was primarily the work of NAMFREL and CARE that provided the necessary field experience and the chief operating personnel out of which this program was ultimately fashioned. The top executive leadership necessary to bring the program into being was supplied by the president of the republic, Ramon Magsaysay, unquestionably one of the greatest Asian leaders of modern times.

He was a relentless foe of communism, an aggressive and powerful fighter for democracy. The central theme in his campaign for the presidency was that if elected he would establish a national program that would "bring the government to the people," and he personally carried that message into every part of the country. In most of the *barrios* the people had never seen a government representative of any kind, but in his own person Magsaysay brought government to life and gave it flesh and blood in the most energetic human form. The name of Magsaysay became magic. Everywhere he went he was worshiped as a hero, a symbol of national pride and expectations, and he was elected by a landslide.

Immediately following his inauguration on December 30, 1953, he began moving to carry out his promise of service to the *barrios,* and a nationwide community development program as an arm of government policy became one of his primary interests. Administrators in agencies throughout the government rose to carry out the president's policy, but they failed to comprehend that a national community development program requires unity and coordination, and that it means much more than an assortment of improvements and independent efforts in various specialized fields of interest.

Community development is concerned not with any one specialized field, but with the community, including all of the functions, activities, facilities, and human attitudes that make for a wholesome and productive place in which to live. It is aimed at building into the community an organization in which the people engage in planning and action to bring about improvement in all aspects of life. It is a comprehensive effort directed toward the creation of thoughts, habits, values, and behavioral patterns that will enable the people to become a self-determining population that will grow continuously in its capacity to deal effectively and constructively with all problems with which it may be confronted.

Because in the early months of Magsaysay's administration, the agencies of the government failed to distinguish between this concept and the ordinary extension of standard government services in agriculture, education, health, social services, and other specialized fields, a major struggle for power was created among the various government services, and the creation of a national community development program was effectively blocked. Within a short time all of the government agencies that had any service of any kind to offer the *barrios* were engaging in an all-out race to outdo each other with the hope of gaining the personal favor of the president. Duplication of effort, overlapping of services, and inter-agency competition grew into a monster which stalked out into the provincial capitals. In the confusion that ensued, pressing needs remained unmet, and very little impact was made on the over-all conditions of life in the *barrios*.

But if there was confusion in the government agencies, there was even more confusion in the communities. People who had never received any service from government found themselves plagued by a proliferation of government agents all wanting to provide some kind of a service, all telling them what they should do, all insisting that their agency was the one to follow, and each disparaging the others.

The Bureau of Agricultural Extension sponsored rural improvement clubs and *barrio* councils. The health people had health councils. The social welfare people had councils. The public school people had councils. As one Filipino put it, "The *barrio* people were being counciled, clubbed, and organized to death by government officials." The effect was that the *barrios* were being torn into so many conflicting pieces by so many competing specialists that no energy was left for a unified community effort. The need for coordination gradually became clear to almost everybody, but each of the competing agencies wanted to be the coordinator.

Finally, in August 1954, in an effort to bring order out of chaos, President Magsaysay issued an executive order creating the Community Development Planning Council (CDPC), composed of the secretaries of a number of the competing departments and three private citizens. The head of the nation's top planning body, the National Economic Council, was designated as chairman. Acting in an advisory capacity only, the CDPC was to devise plans for a coordinated operation that would bring about maximum utilization of all government and private agencies for an integrated national program.

On the advice of Gabriel Kaplan, Magsaysay appointed as executive secretary of the CDPC one of the most extraordinary young men in the Philippines, Ramon P. Binamira, and it was this young man who was to become the principal architect and leader of the Philippine community development program. A better choice could not have been made. In a manner that has been demonstrated in few other countries, Binamira became an illustration of the kind of person that is necessary to establish and make effective a national community development operation. He was brilliant, fearless, direct, and practical. While only twenty-six years old, he had been recruited by Kaplan and Ferrer to head up NAMFREL's community centers project in which he had distinguished himself as a talented organizer and promoter. He had vision and imagination. He was dedicated to the cause of community development and thoroughly understood its philosophy.

From a wealthy family in Cebu, the country's second largest city, he left home at nineteen to begin a successful career in journalism. After two years as publisher of his own newspaper, he decided to study law. At the University of

Southern Philippines, where he was graduated from law school, he became a leader in student politics, and during the election frauds of 1949 was a prominent worker in the Cebu Province campaign to expose corruption.

In 1951, he began his experience with the National Movement for Free Elections by organizing NAMFREL's Cebu chapter and rallying more than thirty thousand young people to watch the polls and help ensure honest voting. During that one year, his life was threatened repeatedly by thugs carrying machine guns, instruments of persuasion almost as frequently used as campaign speeches. One night an armed man went to Binamira's home, climbed a wall of the house and started to lift himself through the window. Binamira placed a carbine at the gunman's head and told him if he did not get down he would blow it off. That ended the threats on Binamira's life, but the enemies of clean elections in Cebu Province never forgot him.

In the 1953 elections which swept Magsaysay into office, Binamira and his friends widened the scope of NAMFREL's activities by organizing chapters all over the central and southern Philippines. Binamira was not a politician and had no political ambitions, but he knew Philippine politics. He was a man of high ethical principle, and was skilled in the art of persuasion.

He took the job as executive secretary of the Community Development Planning Council with high expectations of serving his country but with no idea of the trials and difficulties ahead. For weeks he had no office, no furniture, no equipment, no staff, no budget. He selected three associates who had been experienced in NAMFREL, but he had to go all the way to President Magsaysay to get their appointments cleared through the bureaucracy while they served without pay. And he had to get the president to take personal action to clear his initial budget. Most of his time was absorbed in going from one government office to another explaining what the CDPC was supposed to do.

The heads of the established government departments who were members of the CDPC showed no interest in making it effective, and did not even attend most of its meetings. As a result, the meetings turned out to be little more than academic discussions by the members' alternates who had no power to commit their departments; frequently the meetings were attended by alternates of the alternates. It soon became evident that the only reason the department heads even sent alternates to the meetings was to protect the independent interests of their respective departments and to make sure that Binamira and his staff did nothing that might divert any autonomy or credit away from their agencies. Binamira soon found that although coordination was something everybody was talking about, none of the established government departments had any intention of giving up the slightest bit of their individual authority or of working within the framework of any national plan that might be devised by the CDPC. As the executive secretary of an advisory body which had no sympathy from its own members, Binamira found himself in the position of having no status in the bureaucracy, and without that even a Binamira could not set in motion a national program of community development.

Another major block to the national program, perhaps the most formidable one of all, was the foreign aid mission of the United States government, the USOM, whose technicians, particularly those in agricultural extension, were opposed to the concept of community development. In line with the typical ICA pattern all over the world, these technicians had taught and advocated the splinter approach which had helped create the inter-agency conflict over budgets and program control with which Binamira was now confronted; many of the United States technicians were openly encouraging their Filipino counterparts to resist the coordinated program that was being planned by the Community Development Planning Council.

Still Binamira and his associates did not give up. To demonstrate what a coordinated effort could accomplish, they went out personally and started community development operations in twenty provinces across the country, carefully bringing into the work field agents from the established government agencies. From this they were able within a few months to cite impressive tangible results, and to show how within the framework of comprehensive community development operations the established agencies could accomplish far more in their respective fields of specialization than they could otherwise. But in these efforts Binamira and his men were soon over-extended. They could not establish operations all over the country without a staff of field workers, and they knew that until they could build an agency that would enable them to employ such workers, President Magsaysay's desire for an integrated nationwide program would never be realized.

Meanwhile, there was in the Philippines a man named Y. C. James Yen, a native Chinese educated at Yale and well known for his successful work with peasant villages in China and as the founder of the International Committee of the Mass Education Movement, with headquarters in New York City. He proposed to Magsaysay a plan for a nationwide program in the Philippines similar in some respects to community development, to function outside the structure of government, and to be financed by funds he proposed to raise in the United States. With Magsaysay's written endorsement, Yen succeeded in gaining the support of a powerful group of United States congressmen who pushed through the House of Representatives an amendment to the Mutual Security Act of 1955 authorizing up to 10 per cent of $28.5 million that had been budgeted for aid to the Philippines for a joint commission on rural development—Yen's program. Not only would this program take money away from the budget of the United States foreign aid agency, the ICA, it was to be conducted outside of ICA channels.

Community development had very few friends in the United States aid organization, but something had to be done to stop the "Yen amendment." President Magsaysay was assured that ample funds for community development would be made available through regular ICA channels and that a joint commission of Americans and Filipinos, proposed in the amendment, would damage Philippine-American relations. On this basis Magsaysay agreed to withdraw his support from Yen's efforts in the United States Congress, and the amendment was dropped. But ICA now had to support community development in the Philippines whether its established technical branches liked it or not. From that point on planning for the national program moved swiftly, and in December 1955, a Philippine community development program was formally approved in Washington with an ICA pledge of $4.2 million for the first five years.

That same month President Magsaysay made the final move that was necessary to clear the way. On Christmas Eve he told Binamira that he was interested in only one thing—action. He wanted no more Community Development Planning Council. He wanted no committee of any kind. Binamira alone would be responsible to the president himself for the conduct of community development in the Philippines. A few days later Magsaysay issued Executive Order No. 156, abolishing the Community Development Planning Council, and creating the Presidential Assistant on Community Development (PACD) with broad powers to employ a field staff and to act. Binamira was at last in a position to begin building the national program.

To help organize and manage the affairs of the PACD, Binamira brought in the three men who had been with him in the Community Development Planning Council—a former practicing attorney, a former insurance salesman, and a former school teacher. All of them were thoroughly experienced in the NAMFREL community centers, and shared Binamira's dedication to the objectives of PACD.

From their experience with NAMFREL, Binamira and his associates had learned that the rural people could not be counted upon to come in from the *barrios* to take part in instructional and planning sessions at a central location with sufficient frequency to build support for a solid, long-range development movement. Moreover, it was impossible even when people did come in for such meetings to generate the degree of enthusiasm and community spirit that was necessary to build a major nationwide effort. Therefore, one of the basic principles of the PACD was to start community development operations in the *barrios* where the people actually lived, working on a *barrio*-by-*barrio* basis, and developing citizen initiative and responsibility at that level.

With this principle in mind, Binamira began preparations for a program of recruitment and training that would provide him with a corps of community development field agents who could move into the individual *barrios* and set up a unified, communitywide citizens' organization. The kind of staff he needed could involve no partisan political appointments, and so in January 1956, he arranged for the Bureau of Civil Service to offer an examination for community development workers and to solicit applicants for employment. He appointed a committee at the University of the Philippines to draft a plan of basic training, and using facilities of the university's College of Agriculture, in a rugged natural setting about an hour's drive from Manila, he established a national community development training center.

To explain how the national program would work, he conducted a meeting with the president's cabinet which Magsaysay personally arranged. He held regional seminars with provincial governors and other high government officials for four days each. This was the first time that any real thinking had been devoted to the concept of community development by a substantial number of officials at these levels, and the response in all of these meetings was enthusiastic. Binamira suddenly found himself in the position of having to hold the officials back until he could get his field workers recruited and trained. President Magsaysay himself, impatient for action, was somewhat reluctant to wait for the training, but Binamira stood firm on the principle that the community development program would fail without a well-selected and well-trained corps of field workers.

From his personal knowledge of *barrio* conditions and his experience with the bureaucracy and with Philippine politics,

Binamira had acquired very definite ideas about the kind of people he would need to build a hard-hitting corps of field workers, for he was well aware of the formidable problems they would confront once they got into actual field operations.

"Community development," he said, "is the war against poverty, ignorance, disease, and economic and social stagnation, and we must carry out this program with the same fervor and skill with which we would fight an actual war."

He foresaw the obstacles they faced—the basic difficulties of inducing constructive change in an old civilization, and the politicians and bureaucrats, domestic and foreign, who would view the PACD as a threat to their personal interests and who would not hesitate to destroy it if given a chance.

"We must realize," he said to his associates, "that constantly we are surrounded by enemies. The minute we forget that we are dead."

To Binamira, community development was no mere technique or routine operation, but was potentially capable of shattering the forces of rot within the society so that the wholesome qualities of democracy could grow. He knew that in this kind of an operation opposition and conflict were inevitable, and he was determined not to be deluded by the enthusiasm of the honeymoon period.

"One of the primary requirements of a community development worker," he said, "is the ability to absorb heat. If he fries under heat from those who will attempt to use the program for personal or partisan gain, or who would divert it from its central purpose of strengthening democracy, we don't want him. These are not things you find in textbooks, but are some of the practical facts we must teach our workers, and are some of the reasons we must take pains to select the right people."

Binamira was adamant about the kind of person he needed for PACD's chief training officer. The advisors at USOM and several Filipino professors suggested a person far too academic to meet Binamira's specifications. This key post went to Antonio A. Perpetua, an experienced worker from NAMFREL's community centers who had once been a policeman and who made his way through law school by attending night classes. Perpetua had enormous drive and social consciousness. He was quiet, but highly skilled in organizing and working with groups, and from diligent study on his own he knew community development in both theory and practice.

Binamira and his associates then laid down the criteria to be applied in the selection of all PACD personnel. Foremost, they would seek people of deep personal conviction toward the spirit and purpose of community development. They wanted workers who would not be run over, or as Binamira put it, "swamped" by the recognized technicians of the established government agencies and the USOM.

"We must have community development workers," he said, "who are strong enough to stand up to these technicians and foreign advisors and work with them as equals. Otherwise our people will not command the personal respect they must have to do effective work and to obtain the cooperation they will need from politicians and other government personnel. I will not permit PACD workers to become errand boys for government technicians. The community development program is a partnership matter and that is the way we intend to run it."

Binamira repeatedly pointed out that essentially PACD was dealing with human attitudes which would spell progress or stagnation in the *barrios* where the majority of Filipinos live, and that this required a very high caliber of field agent.

"Our people must be self-starters," he said. "They must be high spirited and self-assertive, yet know when not to assert themselves. They must recognize the importance of emotion and inspiration in what makes human beings tick. They must have drive, courage, freshness, and tact. They must be experts in convincing the *barrio* people that by their own efforts the people can solve most of their problems. They must have faith in people, but be smart enough not to be fooled too often. They must have the type of personality that makes it possible for them to develop within the people the qualities of initiative and leadership that we must have in all our communities to make democracy powerful in this country."

He saw the job of community development with a depth of understanding that few people have achieved. He strongly disagreed with those who looked upon it in mild and theoretical terms. He insisted that PACD trainees should be "noisy, cocky, and aggressive." He described the PACD as an organization that must be made up of "peaceful bandits." He wanted workers who would approach the job with a missionary zeal, but who would be practical and able to operate under the most trying conditions.

To make sure he got them, he laid down an extremely rigid set of conditions for employment. These requirements have been strictly observed from the beginning. Candidates must be college graduates or have experience that can be accepted as equivalent. They must pass a civil service examination designed to measure aptitude and personality traits, and undergo an intensive personal interview before a board of examiners. An average of only two to three out of every one hundred who apply are accepted for training.

Those who are accepted must be willing to train for six months without pay, agree to at least two years of service, and accept assignment anywhere in the country. During training the PACD provides room and board and a stipend of about thirty pesos per month. The training period is a part of the selection process, and a trainee may be dropped at any time if he fails to maintain expected standards of performance.

All trainees first spend two weeks in the *barrios* digging ditches, improving roads, building fences, planting rice, cutting weeds, and doing other physical labor that will give them a personal feeling of the hard life of the *barrio* people. This is also a test of their willingness to work with their hands in *barrio* action projects. A good community development worker must not hesitate to get himself dirty by pitching in with the *barrio* people in projects that involve physical labor. This is one of the important ways of establishing rapport with the people and helping to build civic spirit. Both men and women trainees go through this initial orientation. Trainees then spend a week observing community development organizational activities, and are then given sixteen to eighteen weeks of basic theory training at the resident center. Following this there are two weeks of apprenticeship activities, then two weeks back at the resident center for summary and evaluation. At graduation those who have been successful receive diplomas, a six-months' probationary appointment, and assignment to a post of duty. If they have proved themselves effective organizers and leaders with the *barrio* people by the end of their probation, their appointment becomes absolute; they become full-fledged members of what is probably the most elite organization of civil servants in all Asia.

All members of the PACD from top to bottom have gone through this arduous initiation. Binamira refuses to have supervisors who know less about the art of community development than those working under them—as is frequently the case in other countries. Promotion is based strictly on performance, not on educational background. Salaries are in line with those of other government agencies, but the basic motivation of the PACD is dedication to the task at hand.

One of the keys to the success of PACD training has been that unlike community development planners in many countries, Binamira carefully mapped out an advance plan of field operations so that before the training sessions began he and his associates had a clear picture of the work the field agents were to perform and of the skills they would need. In the light of experience, this plan has been modified in certain details, but in broad outline it is the same today as it was in the beginning.

Each community worker lives in one of the *barrios* and covers five or six neighboring *barrios,* with the responsibility of developing in each *barrio* a citizens' organization through which the majority of the people are taught, led, and stimulated to analyze their local conditions, identify and comprehend their problems, and take action to enrich and improve all facets of their community life—social, cultural, economic, and political. Through this organization thoughts, attitudes, and habits are infused into the population that cause the people to grow in responsibility and civic consciousness and to become increasingly skillful and articulate in recognizing their opportunities and limitations, in making judgments and decisions, in choosing leaders, and in the art of engaging intelligently and effectively in public affairs. The plan is designed to create a ferment of democratic civic activity throughout the nation by uniting the people in constructive planning and action and by building a spirit of cooperation —an atmosphere of willingness and desire to engage in developmental activities that will lead to the achievement of goals the people themselves have determined and for which they are willing to work.

The community worker serves as a personal stimulator and consultant to the people. He does not act as a specialist in anything except community development. He is a general practitioner in the art of motivation, organization, planning, civic action, and leadership. He acts as a direct liaison between the people and the government—interpreting to the government the wishes and needs of the people, and interpreting to the people the policies, intentions, and limitations of the government, with the result that the workings of government are increasingly understood by the people and are increasingly focused to reflect the thoughts and wishes of an informed public. Through the community development operations the Philippine public is becoming a part of the political life of the nation and the desired flow of competent democratic leaders from the bottom up has been set in motion.

Within the framework of the citizens' organization, specialists in agriculture, public health, and other fields are brought into the *barrios* to supply technical information needed to help the people carry out specific improvement projects. The community worker must know when these technicians are needed, be expert at timing their arrival, at creating the best possible conditions under which to bring them in, and at cultivating in the minds of the people the knowledge and enthusiasm that will result in maximum utilization of what the technicians have to offer. Thus, a conscious effort is made to avoid having the work of the technicians result in a mere scattering of assorted village projects that have no relationship to each other in the minds of the people and which therefore become no more than ends in themselves. Instead, the work of the technicians is introduced within the context of an organized communitywide effort that makes it possible to use each village project to contribute toward building and strengthening the forward motion of the citizens' organization. In the process of the operation, the people are taught to recognize that it is through organized community effort that they are able to achieve goals which have importance to them, and that the thing which is of basic significance is not material improvements in themselves, but the democratic organizational machinery that makes it possible for the people to accomplish many improvements and to engage in an increasingly satisfying way in the political and social life stream of the nation.

Binamira repeatedly emphasizes that the primary objective of the community worker is the development of community—the formation of a pattern of attitudes and civic performance that will make it possible to implant a vigorous democracy into the life of the nation. Village projects of an economic and material nature have an essential role in this process, but from the viewpoint of community development these projects are simply a part of the fuel used to build the organizational and institutional foundations prerequisite to a democracy in which citizens can become increasingly adept at making use of their human and natural resources.

To further strengthen the institutional basis for a democratic life, Binamira adopted as one of PACD's chief objectives the development of local autonomy. Never in Philippine history had there been any means of self-government at the *barrio* level where most Filipinos live. A step was made in that direction when in 1955 an act was passed for the establishment of legal *barrio* councils, but this provided little more than advisory powers, and before the operations of the PACD most people were not even aware of the law. As a firmer idea was gained as to the kind of local government that was needed, Binamira and his associates realized the necessity of getting a new law passed by the Philippine Congress that would give the *barrios* true local autonomy and thereby remove a legal block that for hundreds of years had impeded the development of self-determination among the majority of the Filipino people.

"Our aim," said Binamira, "is to change the face of democracy in this country so that we can honestly release the energies of our *barrio* people."

In his usual direct manner he assembled a group of political scientists, senators, and congressmen to draft the needed legislation. The idea was publicized throughout the islands and on January 1, 1960, the *Barrio* Charter Act, one of the most revolutionary documents in current Asian history, became law. This act provides for a legal structure which has now become the core for the *barrio* citizens' organizations. It enables the *barrios* to incorporate, provides for a *barrio* assembly consisting of all legal residents twenty-one years of age and older, an elected chief executive called the *barrio* lieutenant, and an elected *barrio* council. It empowers the *barrios* to raise funds by contributions and to levy their own taxes. They are entitled to 10 per cent of the local real estate taxes that go to the higher governmental levels, and have legal authority generally to manage their local affairs.

To integrate the efforts of the *barrio* people into the operations of government at all levels, community development councils have been established in municipalities throughout the nation (political units similar to United States counties), in all provincial capitals, and at the national level in Manila. These councils are made up of elected public officials, executives of government agencies, and leading private citizens. They make policy, coordinate all government agencies whose services are needed in the program, pass on applications for financial or material assistance, and help promote the community development operations. This system of councils provides a two-way channel of communications between people and government so that the services and material resources of government at all levels may be planned, budgeted, and administered to fit as nearly as possible the technical and material requirements of the field operations. In his capacity as Presidential Assistant on Community Development, Binamira serves as chairman of the coordinating council at the national level, with the provincial governors and municipal mayors chairing the councils at their respective levels and with a PACD staff supervisor serving as executive secretary.

To make it possible for the *barrio* citizens to carry out physical improvements that would otherwise be impossible, and as an added stimulant to the people's efforts, the PACD has established a program of grants-in-aid in which assistance in the form of materials and equipment is supplied to the *barrios*. This aid is granted on a priority basis in accordance with national development goals, and is approved only for those projects the people have carefully thought out in their community development planning, and for which they are willing and able to contribute at least 50 per cent of the cost in cash, materials, or labor. Aid is granted for projects that are considered reasonable, that the people could not accomplish entirely on their own, and that they guarantee to complete and maintain. Applications for this aid are presented by the *barrio* councils, with the technical assistance necessary to figure costs and feasibility being supplied by qualified government technicians.

To ensure the supply of technical services that are needed to backstop work in the *barrios*, roving community development teams have been established throughout the country, each team consisting of an agricultural expert, a veterinarian, a home demonstrator, a public works foreman, a social welfare worker, and a health unit, including a doctor, nurse, midwife, and sanitary inspector. These teams are integrated with the operations of the community development worker and on arrival in a *barrio* are joined by him and the *barrio* school teacher. The members of these teams are not PACD employees, but are provided by other government agencies in the various fields of specialization. Thus, as Binamira has repeatedly emphasized, the PACD is merely one of many agencies engaged in the Philippine community development program, and he insists that proper credit be given to each participating agency. This concept of sharing responsibility and credit in an integrated nationwide effort has been a drastic new departure in Philippine bureaucracy, yet not fully understood, but nonetheless a fundamental part of Philippine community development policy.

Binamira has found that even this carefully organized system is not in itself enough to build the degree of coordination among all units of government that a national program of community development requires. Without the authority vested in him by Magsaysay's executive order which created the PACD, he would not have been able even to organize the system.

"But," he says, "you cannot order the coordination that is needed to make the system work. This can come only from understanding. People cannot be expected to cooperate unless they understand the objectives and methods of community development."

For the purpose of creating this understanding, and with the approval of the national council which is called the Interdepartmental Coordinating Committee, PACD broadened its training operations to offer community development orientation for personnel from all government agencies engaged in the program and for elected officials and leading private citizens. By July 1960, nearly 112,000 people in addition to PACD's own staff had gone though community development training sessions ranging from four-day institutes to six-month courses. This massive training operation has led to the construction at Los Baños of one of the most complete community development training centers in the world, consisting of classrooms, a well-equipped library, an audiovisual room, offices, dormitories, and a combination dining hall and auditorium with seating capacity for five hundred people. At the entrance to the grounds of this center is a sign which reads: "Entering Community Development Center. We Believe in Progress Through Self-Help."

Gradually, the words painted on that sign are beginning to be accepted by the people of the Philippines. Through the PACD system of community development the energies of the people and the resources of government are being harnessed together in a vast nationwide effort that is increasing the effectiveness of both government and people for the development of a nation. At this writing, nearly 1,600 PACD staff members are engaged in intensive citizens' operations in more than 6,300 communities. Local governments have been established in 23,000 *barrios*. Nearly 500 community development coordinating councils are in operation in all of the nation's provinces, with technicians from every nation-building agency in the government participating in the work.

By the end of June 1960, nearly 25,000 grants-in-aid projects had been completed in which each dollar of public funds had resulted in two dollars' worth of improvements, representing an accumulation of rural capital amounting to more than $6 million.

In this island country of Southeast Asia where for generations the majority of the people have lived under conditions as primitive as any in the world, PACD is promoting what many observers have called a peaceful revolution. Because of community development, thousands of peasants are beginning to control plant and animal disease, use selected seed, and grow top-quality crops, poultry, and livestock. They are building food processing plants and small manufacturing enterprises and establishing modern oyster farms. They are building roads and bridges that are increasing by many times the value of their agricultural labors and linking isolated *barrios* with the nation. They are building schools, health centers, sanitary water systems, and scores of other improvements. These material gains achieved by people who earn less in a year than most United States government clerks make in a month is a demonstration of what can be accomplished by investing funds for nation-building purposes within the framework of a nationwide community development operation.

According to an ICA report dated July 1, 1960, the total PACD budget for everything, including grants-in-aid, for four and a half years of operation from January 1956, through June 30, 1960, was 22,181,000 pesos. A little more than half this amount came from the sale of United States surplus commodities in the Philippines. The balance was appropriated by the Philippine Congress. In addition to this peso cost, ICA invested during this period about $1.18 million worth of aid in the form of vehicles and other commodities, and in salaries and expenses for United States personnel—an average of a little more than $262,000 per year. It is doubtful that any organization in the world has made it possible for the American taxpayer to make as much impact for freedom with as few foreign aid dollars as the PACD.

This is due largely to Binamira's policy of using material assistance as he uses everything else—to generate a desire within the people to help themselves. As he puts it, "The lazy can rot." More specifically it is due to the understanding of Binamira and his associates that the basic purpose of community development is not to make material improvements, but to build democracy.

Community development in the Philippines has not turned out to be a panacea any more than it has anywhere else in the world. Despite the dedication and intelligence of Binamira and his associates, their precautionary measures to select and train personnel, and their willingness to be self-critical, it has not yet been possible to build a staff that is uniformly capable of exercising the skills that are required to achieve the goals of community development. Some who have not understood the true meaning of community development have said that it is too slow, that the only way to make the changes that are needed in the underdeveloped parts of the world is for government simply to step in and do it.

To this Binamira says, "There is no other way than community development. You have to learn to walk before you can run. Unless the people from the bottom up go through the process of learning how to use their own intelligence to improve conditions for themselves, no real improvement will ever be made. It is possible that physical amenities could be constructed more quickly by contractors and engineers. And we must do some of this. But you cannot develop a country by physical improvements alone because when you do, you do not develop community. Whatever else you might do to develop a nation there is no short cut to the values that arise from the experience people gain in community development. There is no substitute—except the end of freedom."

On a hot day in June 1960, I rode in a jeep with two community development workers along a dusty road in Luzon, bordered on both sides by thick, tropical jungle. The steady whine of insects filled the air.

"I am a family man," said Irineo. "I took the six-month training with no pay. It was hard, but I want to do this work. Sometimes I would like to rest, on Saturday or Sunday, but you cannot rest and work for PACD because if our program fails it will be because we fail. It is our duty to see that it does not fail."

The other PACD man seemed anxious to speak. His name was Rubero. "There is nothing secure about PACD," he said. "If we do not do a good job, it deserves not to last. If we fail no one can be blamed but us. But I am optimistic. We can make this program permanent, and we will. Maybe we won't be here. But the program will be. No sensible congressman can vote against success."

The sun seemed to get hotter. Bright colored carts lined the road as we neared the municipal center. It was Saturday afternoon. All government offices were closed except PACD.

Irineo said, "None of us would ever let down our chief, Mr. Binamira. But if we did," he chuckled fondly, "he would skin us alive."

At the Community Development Center at Los Baños

where PACD workers are called in periodically for refresher training, there is a large cloth banner embroidered with the words:

> That I shall seek no better
>   reward
> Than to see the happiness of my
>   people and
> The progress of my country.

Beside the words is a fighting cock, a familiar animal that will fight to the death—and the official symbol of PACD.

Says Binamira: "You cannot be soft and run a community development organization."

6

DESPITE ALL OBSTACLES

A FUNDAMENTAL PURPOSE OF COMMUNITY DEVELOPMENT in the underdeveloped parts of the world is to create a self-determining society in which the citizenry as a whole can and will exercise a constructive and productive role in the life of the nation, and to help bring about by peaceful means whatever social, political, and economic changes may be needed to make this kind of a society possible. It must be anticipated that any program that is successful in achieving this purpose, or which shows signs of becoming successful, is likely to encounter hostility and opposition.

Much of this opposition will be based on misunderstandings growing out of the fact that community development represents a departure from long established practices, but it will also come from groups and individuals who will interpret a program of this kind as a threat to their personal interests. One of the most important considerations that must therefore be taken into account in planning a national community development program is how to unite the major national forces in the effort in order to prevent or reduce the possibility of opposition, how to deal with opposition if it appears, and how to obtain as the national leader of the program an individual who has the personal qualities to meet this problem courageously and effectively.

The Philippines is perhaps the outstanding example in the world of how this opposition can assert itself, and of the action and leadership that must be exercised to deal with it in order to establish the program on a firm operating basis. The story of opposition to the Philippine program, and of the counteraction that was taken to overcome it under the leadership of Ramon P. Binamira, has also become a dramatic illustration of the impact that community development may have for the building of political responsibility among the masses in a country where the great mass of the population has never before exercised such responsibility. For that reason, I shall tell this story here in detail.

Scattered over the Philippines are short bits of unfinished paved roads that begin at no particular point and lead to no particular place, the silent reminders of a well-established pork barrel system long used by Philippine congressmen as one of their most effective vote-getting weapons. Under this system the Philippine Congress places public works funds at the disposal of its members to use as they see fit. Road engineers are notified by the congressmen where to build in their respective districts, whom to hire, when to start, and when to stop, and unless a community guarantees to vote "right" it need not expect consideration when the pork barrel pie is sliced. Conveniently, most pork barrel projects are allocated only a short time before election when congressmen are most anxious to hire large numbers of people; they usually close down shortly after election and never quite seem to get finished. There is probably no country in the world that has exceeded the Philippines in the use of politics for the personal welfare of politicians.

Having grown accustomed to this time-honored system, many Filipino politicians found it difficult to adopt a friendly attitude toward a government program that dealt directly with the people in the intimate manner of the PACD and which was rapidly building a thinking and articulate mass citizens' organization. With people in community development building and completing roads at about one-fifth the normal cost, and with enlightened civic attitudes beginning to take root in the population mass, there was reason to fear that a political reform was in the making that would plug the holes in the public treasury and seriously upset the lush practices that had long been open to politicians.

As the PACD spread its operations over the country, the pressure to use the program for political patronage and partisan gain steadily mounted and the conflict that Binamira had foreseen became intense. He knew that if he or any of his people ever yielded to this pressure their effectiveness as agents of community development would be finished, but in resisting the pressure he made some determined political enemies. He always knew that he could completely count on the support of President Magsaysay; but suddenly and without warning, Magsaysay was removed from the scene of action.

On March 16, 1957, Binamira flew to his home town of Cebu with President Magsaysay in the president's private plane. They were due to return to Manila that night, but at the last minute Binamira decided to stay over a day or two longer. In the early morning darkness of the Seventeenth the president's plane took off. Nine minutes later it crashed into Mt. Manunggal, and all passengers were killed. Thus ended the life of Ramon Magsaysay, the man who had made possible the Philippine community development program, and who from the beginning had provided it with an umbrella of protection.

Binamira hurried back to Manila, resignation in hand, to Carlos P. Garcia, the former vice president. It was Binamira's feeling that his offer of resignation was only proper courtesy. But President Garcia did not want him to leave.

Binamira agreed to stay, but only on the condition that the PACD not be used for partisan political purposes, and that its program continue unchanged. President Garcia agreed to these conditions and issued the first official policy statement of his administration.

Dated March 29, 1957, it read:

Immediately upon my assumption of office as President, I committed myself unequivocally and without any reservation to the continuation of the policies of the late President Ramon Magsaysay.

With specific reference to the Magsaysay Community Development Program, I wish to declare that this Program, without any changes, will receive my direct and personal attention and that its implementation, through the Office of the Presidential Assistant on Community Development, will be pursued with greater vigor and determination by my Administration.

A few days later sixty-three congressmen signed a petition to oust Binamira from office, but Garcia quietly refrained from taking action. As knowledge of the petition spread through the provinces the political potential of community development flared into angry reality.

Letters and telegrams, resolutions from provincial boards, statements from governors, mayors, and *barrio* leaders supporting Binamira came in such numbers and in such strong language as to cause most of the congressmen who had signed the petition to deny even that they had done so. Others, when confronted in person and asked for an explanation, said they had not read the petition and did not know that it concerned Binamira. Within a short time the matter was dropped, but the pressures continued to mount.

One of his bitterest enemies, a congressman who was a leader in the political machine in Cebu Province where Binamira's life had been threatened during the fight for clean elections, charged Binamira with misuse of PACD funds. As soon as these charges were disproved, Binamira's enemies resorted to other tactics.

For a period of 120 days prior to the general elections of 1957, PACD was prohibited from spending any funds appropriated by Congress that year for *barrio* projects; and to compound the difficulties, Binamira's enemies managed to get him embroiled in weeks of legal wrangling as to whether PACD could operate at all during that period, or even pay its employees. He no sooner passed this crisis than others arose.

In 1958, a powerful congressman took action to block the entire PACD budget by having it removed from the congressional budgetary schedules. After considerable maneuvering Binamira managed to get this action retracted. A short time later he received a call directing him to appear before a conference of congressmen who were meeting to discuss the budgets of several government agencies. There he was instructed in blatant terms to issue a letter to all of the slightly more than seven hundred field agents he had at that time, terminating their services, regardless of civil service status, and to submit by noon the following day signed blank appointment forms for the congressmen to fill as they saw fit with the names of their political proteges. Binamira asked if the congressmen realized that the government had already spent 1.5 million pesos to train these field workers, and that without trained personnel the community development program would fail. But reason was of no value. The sole interest of the congressmen was how many jobs PACD could supply for political patronage.

The next day Binamira delivered to the House a letter stating that he would not comply with the congressmen's instructions, and orally made it clear that if the threat were carried out he would reveal the matter publicly. Another crisis was dispelled, but hardly a week passed without his being subjected to some kind of political harassment. Frequently, the obstructions he had to put up with bordered on the burlesque, but each time he managed to keep the program operating despite the valuable time these difficulties took away from productive work.

Knowing that when the PACD budget came up before the Senate Appropriations Committee in the 1960 session of Congress he could expect opposition from a senator who had been involved in the infamous election frauds and terrorism of 1949, Binamira prepared for the hearing by moving two truckloads of papers on community development projects in the senator's home province into the hearing room, and covering the walls with project photographs.

At the hearing the senator, operating according to expectations, said that he had never seen a PACD pig, and that the organization should be dissolved.

Holding in his hand a picture of a pig from one of the community development projects in the senator's district, Binamira said, "Senator, will you look at this picture carefully?"

"Yes," said the senator.

"When you look at this pig," said Binamira, "it looks like any other pig, doesn't it?"

"Yes."

"Two ears?"

"Yes."

"Two eyes?"

"Yes."

"Four feet?"

"Yes."

"That's right, Mr. Senator," said Binamira. "This is a PACD pig, and it looks like any other pig. We haven't been able to invent one that has a different appearance. It is not possible for you to recognize a PACD pig from any other pig, except perhaps it is larger, because these are pure breeds."

Then Binamira pointed to the two truckloads of papers which had made a considerable mountain in the room. Those papers, he informed the senator, were all from community development projects in his district. He invited the senator to select any paper and he would personally take the senator out to see for himself that the project existed.

"Do your people have civil service eligibility?" asked the senator.

"Mr. Senator," said Binamira, "all my people have eligibility beginning with myself, even in two cases where the job does not require eligibility." He handed the senator a list of all PACD employees with their eligibility ratings.

The senator sat for about fifteen minutes looking through the list, and finally said he had no more questions.

But Binamira was soon busy with another crisis.

One hour before the bill containing his budget for the 1960-1961 fiscal year was scheduled to be brought before the Senate, he learned that someone had surreptitiously placed two brackets around a critical section of the bill which had the effect of killing that section. Binamira rushed to the Senate floor just in time to get permission to retype the pages that had been affected, have them mimeographed, distributed to the senators, and included in the bill as it was finally passed.

These are but a few examples of the obstacles Binamira had to fight to prevent the PACD from being destroyed once its field operations were set in motion. Meanwhile, he had to keep himself equally occupied fighting other attempts to destroy it that were made by United States foreign aid officials in the Philippines mission of the ICA, the USOM. Most of the attacks launched by Filipinos did not begin until after the death of Magsaysay, but the harassment from ICA officials began even before Magsaysay was killed. The "Yen amendment" and President Magsaysay's personal determination had caused the ICA to contribute financial support to community development in the Philippines, but that did not mean that the specialized sections of ICA in Washington or their USOM representatives in Manila had accepted it. From the time PACD began its operations in 1956 a core of USOM technicians carried on a steady campaign to discredit the program and prevent it from succeeding.

When PACD was established, ICA had no community development division in its Philippines mission, and there was no United States technician in Manila who had been trained or experienced in community development work. Binamira formally requested that such a division be established, and after months of delay this was accomplished. But the resistance continued.

An ICA official who was neutral described the situation this way:

This idea of community development did not originate with ICA and our technicians never understood what it meant. Our agricultural people fought it from the beginning, as they have all over the world. They saw it as a threat to agricultural extension because it was different from anything they had experienced. They were afraid it would overshadow them, and they were irked over the fact that community development was getting job positions they wanted.

A Filipino official put it this way:

It was a sneaking suspicion that as community development got going it would gobble up the functions of some of the established agencies and run them out of business. There was no need for that suspicion because from the outset community development demonstrated that it would make these agencies more important instead of less important, but the ICA technicians couldn't understand that. To them it was kill or be killed.

This resistance grew to such proportions that it became necessary for Binamira to have the president of the republic request that the American official who was leading the campaign be removed from the country within twenty-four hours or he would be formally declared *persona non grata* by the government of the Philippines. This ultimatum was confirmed by a written communication dated June 20, 1958, addressed to the ICA mission director in Manila, which read in part as follows:

> . . . I have been informed by the Presidential Assistant on Community Development, Mr. Ramon P. Binamira, that in spite of the advances made by this project [the community development program], it has suffered greatly from active opposition within the Philippine Department of Agriculture . . . we are greatly disturbed to learn that this opposition has been fomented directly by . . . the Chief of the Agriculture Division of the local ICA Mission. Since this project was started . . . [he] has consistently and actively engaged in a campaign to crystalize opposition and to negate this program. . . .
>
> Since the Community Development Project is strongly supported by both the Philippine and United States Governments, it is indeed unfortunate that an advisor within the International Cooperation Administration should have beliefs contrary to the President's Program on Community Development. We hope, therefore, that you will agree with us that under these conditions we have no alternative but to request the International Cooperation Administration to assign . . . [him] to a place other than the Philippines where his personal belief is not inconsistent with the policy laid down by the host country.
>
> Very sincerely yours,
JUAN C. PAJO
Executive Secretary
Office of the President of the Philippines

"It was an unfortunate incident," said Binamira, "but it had to happen. In my travels around Asia I had seen cases in other countries where ICA agricultural advisors were deliberately trying to scuttle community development programs. I saw it in Pakistan. I saw it in India, in Iran, and in Korea. There was nothing personal in our case. It was an attitude in ICA that we could not change, but we could not afford to let it scuttle our program in the Philippines."

Faced by Binamira's continuous vigilance, the opposition within ICA gradually withered. The Philippines became known as one country in which foreign officials unfriendly to community development were not wanted, and as these officials were replaced, there emerged in the USOM a group of advisors who were genuinely dedicated to the success of the program. Two of these advisors who deserve special credit were Richard V. Bernhart, who became USOM's chief community development advisor, and Harry N. Naylor, a distinguished anthropologist who contributed significantly to establishing in the University of the Philippines the Community Development Research Council which has been of invaluable service to the operating program.

It should be emphasized that the program in the Philippines would not have been possible without ICA financial support. However, the kind of foreign aid that PACD really needed in addition to financial support, as have all other community development programs in the world, was a warm friendly ally, a sympathetic, enthusiastic, imaginative, and intelligently critical fellow promoter. The PACD was fortunate in having this kind of help from certain individuals such as Gabriel L. Kaplan in his capacity as a private advisor, such as Edward R. Chadwick of the United Nations, and from several individuals in the USOM. But despite the personal support of a few individuals, the leaders of the PACD knew that the general coolness of the ICA toward the concept of community development never really changed.

Due primarily to the personal leadership of Binamira and his associates and to the growing support of other enlightened Filipino leaders, along with large numbers of the citizenry, the PACD is still a major force for democratic vitality and socio-economic progress in the Philippines. But the struggle for survival is yet to be won. In its underlying foundation, the PACD has one serious weakness. Its legal basis for existence is an executive order that was issued by a man who died in 1957. This means that the sole legal authority for the PACD's continuation could be canceled by the stroke of one man's pen, or the Philippine Congress has only to draw a line through an item on the national budget page.

In 1960 at a conference of provincial governors and other high officials, a resolution was passed to eliminate this weakness by congressional action that would make the PACD a permanent administration with statutory authority, and Binamira was asked to draft a bill. With this move the enemies of the program loomed larger than ever. Binamira's steady refusal to yield to political pressure to convert the program into pork barrel or allow it to be used for patronage or other partisan purposes had resulted in a hard core of congressional resistance. In the face of this hostility the PACD bill was drafted, and in 1961 was introduced in the Philippine Congress.

At that time the Nacionalista Party of President Garcia and its leading opposition, the Liberal Party, were readying themselves for a general election. Widespread accusations of corruption and negligence were being leveled at the Garcia administration. Significantly, support for PACD and its program of community development was made a major campaign promise by both parties, but as the political tensions mounted in intensity the PACD found itself in an extremely difficult position. If it kept out of the campaign, it was certain to arouse the hostility of the Nacionalistas who then controlled Congress and hence the fate of the PACD bill. The Nacionalistas not only wanted to claim credit in the campaign for the creation of the PACD, they wanted to use its organization and its funds to help win the campaign. Still, Binamira stood by his convictions and PACD remained neutral. To the Nacionalistas this was bad enough, but to make matters worse, the honesty and dedication to public service which had brought Binamira and his organization respect throughout the nation were held up in the press as an outstanding exception to the alleged corruption of the Garcia government.

The PACD bill was thrown into a Nacionalista Party caucus where nine congressmen succeeded in getting it bottled up in the House Rules Committee. Throughout the nation, mass public rallies were held in support of the bill, posters urging its passage dotted the landscape, hundreds of thousands of people rose to its defense, including governors, mayors, and other public leaders. But the bill struck at the very roots of the congressional patronage system, and the hard core of politicians who were determined to perpetuate that system had no intention of allowing the measure to get through unless Binamira was willing to compromise his principles. The bill died without a vote.

A few days later an editorial in Manila's *Evening News* reported that PACD personnel had been accused of being pro-Liberal. "This is most unfortunate," said the editorial. "Even if it were true that PACD employees are pro-Liberal —and this is highly doubtful since one of the reasons for the success achieved by the organization is its single-minded determination to keep itself above politics and partisan considerations—there is no question that it is doing excellent work and should stop being dependent on foreign doles for its continued existence.

"It is regrettable that the whole program of community development should be imperilled simply because some congressmen cannot see beyond narrow partisan considerations. It is regrettable because it shows only too clearly that far too many of our congressmen have what, for lack of a better name, we could call the 'pork barrel mentality.'

"In other words," the editorial continued, "they want to be sure that every government office created should be willing to take in their proteges or that every successful project should be credited to them. But the PACD, through its chief, Ramon Binamira, has been singularly uncooperative in this respect. The PACD has divorced itself from politics, adhered to the civil service, and resisted all efforts to make it the dumping ground of political misfits.

"Let our congressmen realize for once that the Philippines will never progress unless the folk in the *barrios* and villages are taught to help themselves. Let them see the grave injustice they are doing to the Filipino people by shelving the PACD bill. Then, let them reconsider their action. It is not yet too late."

The editorial was right, it is not too late. For despite the vast progress yet to be made, democracy in the Philippines is on the march, largely because of the PACD. An Association of Barrio Councils representing millions of people engaged in community development is spreading support for the movement throughout the country; the League of Provincial Governors and City Mayors and powerful national leaders, including many senators and congressmen, are solidly behind the work. In November 1961, more than seven million voters turned out at the polls and elected Diosdado Macapagal, leader of the Liberal Party, as the new president of the republic and Emmanuel Pelaez as the new vice president. Both of them are on record as supporters of the PACD, determined to insulate it against political encroachments in order to safeguard the spirit of self-help it is generating in thousands of *barrios* on virtually every inhabited island where countless numbers of men and women are beginning to see new hope for the future.

Today the people of the Philippines are demonstrating what a national program of community development can mean. They are doing it with courage and intelligence. They are setting an example of how democracy can be built against vast obstacles in the Asian world. It can only be hoped that whatever forces needed to keep the movement alive will be marshaled. For this example is too precious. Filipinos must not let themselves and the rest of the free world be disappointed.

7

TROUBLE IN THE
MIDDLE EAST

IN IRAN, IN THE CRITICAL AND TROUBLED MIDDLE EAST, community development as a nationwide program came about more by coincidence than by design, and as a consequence offers a lesson of far-reaching significance.

Beginning in 1946, the Near East Foundation, a voluntary foreign aid organization of New York, established a comprehensive development program in an area of Iran known as the Varamin Plains not far southeast of Tehran, the national capital. This program was being carried on in cooperation with various ministries of the Iranian government. Operating out of a field headquarters at Mamazon where the Near East Foundation established a teaching center, the program covered a rural area encompassing thirty-five peasant villages in which the people had been living under the same primitive conditions for hundreds of years.

This modest program was being carried out with limited private funds, but it was a bold experiment intended as a pilot demonstration to develop techniques for progress to be applied in rural areas throughout Iran. The Varamin Plains project was not generally called community development at that time, but in essence that is what it was. It was broadly conceived to include all aspects of community life—economic, social, and cultural—and was calculated to generate an organized effort by the people in each village to work for their own improvement with assistance from outside the village. Included in the project were technicians from a variety of specializations all brought together in an integrated effort. The Varamin Plains project of the Near East Foundation was, in short, one of the earliest programs of community development in that part of the world.

During this time social and political upheaval erupted in Iran, growing out of the great surge of Iranian nationalism following World War II and the extended oil dispute with the British. Suddenly, these events in the Middle East became a threat to the peace of the world. In 1950, the United States Congress passed President Truman's Point Four program, and the Iranian government, pushing hard for action that would help bring social reform, was one of the first to apply for Point Four assistance. The Iranian request was received in Washington even before there had been time for the aid program to be organized.

Recognizing the need for a program that would go directly to the people and make a quick impact, a decision was reached in the State Department to capitalize upon the experience of the Near East Foundation and make $50,000 available for the Foundation to expand its efforts in the Varamin Plains. That was early in 1951. Within a few months the State Department came through with another $247,000, and the project was further bolstered by personnel assigned from the Iranian government. In time the Near East Foundation received well over $1 million from United States foreign aid funds.

Meanwhile, the governments of the United States and Iran signed an agreement called Technical Cooperation for Rural Development, and a Joint Commission for Rural Improvement was established to direct the program, but with the Near East Foundation handling the operations in the Varamin Plains on a virtually independent basis. Objectives of the basic agreement between the two governments were, broadly stated, to improve the living conditions of the people in the villages and increase their productivity.

Soon after this agreement was signed a USOM was established in Tehran and United States government representatives began arriving. Included in these early arrivals were a mission director and several consultants who were among the proponents of community development in the foreign aid agency, and who were favorably disposed to community development as it was then beginning to unfold in India. Thus, the term "community development" soon came into broad usage in Iran, and in time the work of the Near East Foundation came to be known by that term.

Another early impetus to community development in Iran came as a result of an edict issued on January 27, 1951, by His Imperial Majesty the Shah, ordering that lands owned by the crown be sold to village peasants for a nominal sum payable over a long period of time; a royal commission was established to carry out the order. This edict was regarded by United States officials as a significant measure of land reform that would help strengthen and stabilize the political structure of Iran by creating the beginning of a land- and home-owning middle class. The edict was also viewed as having major importance internationally because of the proximity of Iran to the Soviet Union, and because of the prestige that the Shah's personal sponsorship gave to the reform. By the same token, it was felt that if this land reform should fail it would damage the prestige of the Shah, and have adverse repercussions throughout the entire Middle East. For these reasons, it was felt that every effort should be made to conduct a program in the villages where crown lands were to be distributed that would adequately prepare the villagers for the successful management of their own farm and village affairs.

To accomplish this action it was decided to set up an organization similar to that which had been worked out in the community development program in India. Using a dozen villages as a pilot development block, the program provided for multi-purpose workers for the villages, a development bank to make credits available to the peasants, and technical assistance from the Ministries of Health, Agriculture, and Education. The Near East Foundation was given funds by the United States government and by the Ford Foundation to train the village workers. Thus, community development was well on its way to being established in Iran under the leadership of the United States foreign aid organization.

But as the standard technical divisions of the USOM began to get organized, increasing confusion as to the meaning of community development began to arise in the minds of many people in Iran—both Americans and Iranians.

Soon a flurry of scattered projects having to do with rural improvement came to be referred to as community development, including several that should have been called something else. Other projects almost identical to some that were being called community development were being operated under quite different names such as fundamental education. All these programs were directed at improving villages, and because most of the United States government employees who were sent to Iran did not understand the difference between community development and a scattering of isolated technical services, the confusion that existed in Washington was transplanted to Tehran and mingled with the confusion that already existed in the Iranian government. Thus, the good start that had been made soon began to deteriorate.

Meanwhile, Prime Minister Mossadegh, who gained power during the surge of Iranian nationalism, was pushing a wide range of reforms, including basic improvements in rural life to be extended to all of Iran's approximately 45,000 peasant villages. For many centuries most Iranian villages and surrounding agricultural lands had been owned by a small landlord class which exercised powerful influence over the economic and political life of the country, and which had traditionally reaped the lion's share of the wealth from village agriculture. It was the depressive effect of this system, which has not changed to this day, that became one of the prime targets of the Mossadegh reforms.

Using extraordinary powers for quick action which he had received from the Iranian Parliament, Mossadegh established a law requiring villages throughout the country to organize village councils, each consisting of a representative of the landlord, a village headman appointed by government authorities, and three peasants elected by popular vote. In February 1953, he put into effect a tax requiring the landlords to pay 10 per cent of their earnings from the land for the councils to use for village improvements, plus an additional 10 per cent to be distributed to the villagers personally. These laws to give the peasants a voice in village affairs, improve the physical conditions, and increase the peasants' share of village agricultural earnings were a part of the revolutionary trend then sweeping not only Iran but the entire Middle East. This action was extremely unpopular with the traditionally dominant landlord class, but was highly popular with the rising new intellectuals and liberals. In government circles these acts were referred to as the community development law and became popularly known as the Mossadegh Law.

On the basis of the Mossadegh Law the United States and Iranian governments created a joint fund for "agrarian development" to help the village councils carry out improvements with the funds they were to get from the landlords. Iran provided ninety million rials (a little less than $1.3 million), and the United States provided $3 million. To provide administrative machinery for this agreement a new Iranian government agency known as the Bongah Emran, or the Community Development Bongah, was established in the Ministry of Interior. The Bongah was to develop the new program countrywide and the Near East Foundation was to hire thirty-one American technicians to advise in the work. In practice the Bongah was under the direction of the USOM and the Near East Foundation.

The agreement for agrarian development was signed on June 28, 1953, only a few months after the landlord tax had gone into effect. Less than two months later Prime Minister Mossadegh who was threatening the power of the Shah, was overthrown by a military *coup d'etat* led by General Zahedi, one of Mossadegh's bitterest enemies whose plot against the prime minister carried the blessings of the Shah.

Suddenly, Tehran was thrown into turmoil. But the outward signs of turmoil were quickly suppressed. General Zahedi was named prime minister, Mossadegh was imprisoned, and the Shah married his daughter to Zahedi's son who was later appointed ambassador to the United States.

It was alleged that Mossadegh had aligned himself with the Communists, and this allegation was given wide currency in other parts of the world, including the United States. This accusation was deeply resented by many informed and patriotic Iranians who pointed out that this accusation was simply a case of confusing communism with legitimate nationalism, and in fact had been cleverly promoted and used by the Communists themselves to discredit Mossadegh. Mossadegh's social reforms were actually a threat to the Communists because had these reforms succeeded, the primary basis for mass discontent which provided the Communists with grist for stirring agitation among the people would have been substantially reduced. The military, on the other hand, had its own grievances against the prime minister. It had the support of the Shah, and it reflected the attitudes of the landlord and wealthy class which saw its traditional position of social and economic dominance threatened. The military therefore had political reasons of its own to discredit Mossadegh and gain control of the government. Thus, it appears that the Communists and the military, although inherent enemies representing opposite extremes, converged in a temporary alliance to achieve a common end —the destruction of Mossadegh.

As the struggle for political power which had gained momentum from the nationalization of British-controlled Iranian oil moved through its final gyrations in the top layer of Iranian society, the vast majority of the people were left in the position of spectators with no actual voice in the outcome. Mossadegh, however, had come to be highly revered by a substantial segment of the Iranian public, particularly within the newly educated classes from which much of the rank and file of government officials and workers had been drawn. And the quality of performance of these people had an important bearing upon the success or failure of actual field operations in the various programs for rural improvement that were being supported by United States foreign aid.

When the political drama then unfolding moved into its climax of a military coup against Mossadegh, a belief grew among Mossadegh's followers that the United States government had assisted in bringing about the demise of Mossadegh whom they regarded as an Iranian national hero. This triggered widespread resentment toward the United States government in Iran, even though the need for economic aid from the United States was generally recognized.

Reacting swiftly to this situation, the tempo of Communist propaganda was intensified, with the USOM, known in Iran as Point Four, as a prime target for the propaganda barrage. Many peasant villages, gripped by illiteracy, disease, poverty, and frustration, were victimized by this propaganda, and their age-old suspicion toward government was thereby deepened. The effect of the Communist propaganda, along with the fall of the Mossadegh government, became so great as to make it necessary in some cases to conceal the United States marking from the doors of vehicles being used in foreign aid projects, and there were instances where leads showing that educational films were presented by United States foreign aid had to be deleted. Many able and educated Iranians who under Mossadegh had been spiritually driven in their work by the ideology of reform now lost interest in their work. Resentful of what Zahedi represented, and believing that his ascent to power had been supported by the administration that had just taken office in Washington, these Iranians felt that the only real hope of a better life for the masses of the Iranian people had been struck down, and that they could not in good conscience go to the villages as representatives of a government under Zahedi. Many sought transfers to positions that were not connected with United States foreign aid programs, in many cases even at half their former salaries. Meanwhile, collections from the Mossadegh Law which had formed the basis for the agra-

rian development project virtually ceased, though even before the *coup d'etat* many landlords had avoided making the
required payments.

However, with the collections that had been made and
the joint fund which had been established by the American
and Iranian governments, the agrarian development project,
referred to as community development, was put into operation. Loan funds and engineering plans and services were
made available. One hundred Iranians, called "community
development specialists," were trained, and in rapid order
thousands of village councils were organized. In approximately three years this nationwide project resulted in con-
structing thousands of physical facilities in the villages and
rural areas, including bath houses, mosques, water supplies,
roads, bridges, and clinics.

But the agrarian development project made little impact
on the basic life conditions or the attitudes of the villagers,
despite the fact that millions of dollars were expended. If
anything, the villagers were made even more dependent.
Although the project was called "community development,"
it was not in reality a community development program. It
was a building and loan operation focused on the construction of public works with much of the construction being
done by paid construction crews and contractors, and with
minor attention being given to the creation of civic effort
and self-reliance, or to true participation by the villagers.

Under the conditions of nationwide frustration and restlessness which the change of government and Communist
propaganda had helped bring about, Iran was then in even
greater need of genuine community development than it had
been before. Community development would have been an
effective means by which the challenge of the times could
have been met, and by which renewed confidence in American aid could have been generated among the people. But
instead, the foreign aid organization pushed the building of
physical projects without giving sufficient thought to the
impression they might make upon the villagers. Reports of
action accomplished had to be sent to Washington.

In many villages the landlords, fearful of the power of education among the people, worked through village priests (whom they also dominated) to convince the people that it was irreligious to do anything other than what the landlords wished. Mosques were frequently built instead of desperately needed schools, and the feeling of subservience which for generations had helped to suppress free expression of thought and opinion among the peasants was played upon and heightened. Attitudes of resentment toward foreigners were enhanced by construction crews and foreign engineers descending on the villages and building installations such as sanitary bathhouses which the villagers did not understand and which no one bothered to explain. Thousands of the village councils were no more than paper organizations, in many cases mere pawns of the landlords. Not only was the agrarian development project not community development, it damaged the reputation of the term community development. But it did give the term wide currency in Iran.

Meanwhile, there were also many other projects referred to as community development, all directed at the villages and their surrounding agricultural lands but without any overall unity. However, despite the waste and disorder that prevailed, some Iranians and Americans saw what could be accomplished if a genuine national community development program could be organized and carried out. The operations of the Near East Foundation in the Varamin Plains continued to illustrate that potential.

After four years of confusion and disorganization, the Bongah was reorganized with a board of directors appointed by the minister of interior and a chief of community development with a field staff in each province of the country. Finally, most of the projects that had been referred to as community development were placed under the Bongah's jurisdiction. Enough public recognition of the need to do something for the village peasants had been stirred up by the Mossadegh Law to make it obvious that some action had to be taken. No effort had been made to enforce this law since Mossadegh's removal from the scene. Therefore, in connection with the reorganization of the Bongah a new community development law was passed. To at least quiet the revolutionary discontent, it was decided to collect 5 per cent of the landlord's income for use in village improvements. However, the village councils were changed to village societies consisting of one representative of the landlord, the village headman (usually another landlord appointee), one peasant popularly elected, and two peasants chosen jointly by the landlord's representative and the elected peasant.

This change in the law demonstrated the renewed power of the landlords and strengthened their control over the village organizations. The only possible way that the peasants could be free to express themselves under this arrangement was by a skillful job of community development through which the village landlords could be led voluntarily to see that their best interests would actually be served by upgrading the conditions of life among the peasants, and honestly encouraging them to express themselves and develop a greater sense of responsibility for village welfare and productivity. A small minority of the landlords have done this and have thereby learned the validity of this principle, but in most cases the ancient pattern of landlord rule and peasant subservience is yet to be changed.

In general, the Bongah was set up along two major lines of operation. The first was to organize village societies over the entire country with a minimum of follow-up until more intensive service could be supplied. This meant, in effect, that whatever community development was accomplished would have to be done through the landlord-controlled village societies with limited guidance from the Bongah. The second major line of operations was an intensive effort in blocks of villages selected in various parts of the country, organized along the lines of the community development program in India. Each development block in Iran was to include from fifty to two hundred villages, with a block officer and a variety of specialists working out of a headquarters, and a staff of village workers called *dehyars,* meaning friends of the village, living and working in the villages. The *dehyars* were to cover all aspects of community life, while the specialists came in to give technical advice in their fields of specialization. The Varamin Plains project was in essence a block development organization. Wherever possible the specialists were supplied by the various ministries; if not, the Bongah hired its own.

In 1956, the Ministry of Interior and USOM entered into a master contract with the Near East Foundation making the Foundation the general advisor for community development in Iran. With this contract signed and the variety of isolated project agreements pulled together in the over-all organization of the Bongah, there was hope that community development might be established on a sound national basis in Iran. Operational procedures were carefully worked out covering all aspects of the Bongah's program—village societies, development blocks, special activities to improve the status of women, housing and engineering services, training in the organization of cooperatives, and services aimed at the development of village industries. Arrangements were made for technical services in health, agriculture, education, and all other essential fields. Machinery for a campaign of public information was established. Recruitment was stepped up, and the Varamin Rural Training Center, with extra financial assistance from the Ford Foundation, was geared to increase the supply of trained workers. Special conferences were held with the representatives of the various government agencies in the provinces to explain the program. Everywhere there was enthusiastic response.

But the organization had no more than been completed and readied for action when serious financial difficulties began to emerge. Arrangements had been made to ensure the payment of American salaries and other contract expenses of the Near East Foundation, but much less definite arrangements had been made for the Bongah and its Iranian employees. The Bongah had not been included in the budget of the Iranian government. Funds from the 5 per cent to be collected from the landlords were slow coming in, and collections were never satisfactory. More than sixty million rials had been left over from the Mossadegh Law, but legal and administrative red tape resulted in many months passing before this money could be used. Some money was available from the separate project agreements previously started by USOM which had been transferred to the Bongah, but a continuous shifting of USOM policy resulted in a gradual drying up of this source of support.

Thus, the Bongah was left in a tenuous position. In Tehran much time had to be devoted to begging for money from whatever sources could be found. It was not always possible even to meet the payroll. While the Americans were being paid regularly the Iranians were going through the experience of payless paydays and having to meet expenses out of their own pockets. To make matters worse, it had been decided that many of the community development workers would have to furnish their own transportation which many of them did not have. Budgets were continuously having to be slashed, people were hired only to be laid off because there was not enough money to pay them, operations were frequently changed, and long-range plans were made and then canceled. Demoralizing rumors and internal friction from operating under a cloud of insecurity became commonplace. Morale sank to a low ebb. Had it not been for the devotion to the cause of community development which many Iranians clearly demonstrated, it is doubtful the Bongah could have survived.

These difficulties were multiplied by the fact that each member of the Bongah's board of directors exercised a hand in the management. Although there was a managing director, he had little more authority than the other directors. And because of the lack of clarity as to the meaning and purpose of community development, many Iranian government agencies viewed the Bongah as a threat to their own separate operations. This problem of inter-agency jealousies and conflicts raged continuously in Tehran; though out in the field where government workers were more directly confronted by the needs of the villages, it was far less serious.

Early in 1957, there was another change in the Iranian

government. The new minister of interior, more influenced by the traditional landlord resistance to agrarian reform than his predecessor, publicly expressed doubts about the Bongah's efficiency and asked the USOM to study the administration of the Bongah.

That same year the USOM completed its study of Bongah administration and attempted to curtail four important functions of the Bongah organization. These were all functions that had been created by the earlier isolated project agreements which had been referred to as community development, and which had wisely been integrated into the over-all operations of the Bongah with the approval of the USOM director.

The functions recommended for elimination from the Bongah included housing and engineering which provided the villages with plans and technical service for the construction of homes, schools, mosques, and other physical facilities which are an integral part of developing communities.

The building of physical improvements does not in itself constitute a community development program, but when such improvements are made within the context of the comprehensive effort which community development entails, they become not only an important part of that effort, they become one of the significant means by which a feeling of achievement is generated among the people, thereby giving impetus to the total process of developing an enriched community life and a viable democracy. When such physical improvements are made as ends in themselves separate and apart from the process of community development—which is normally what happens when they are promoted separately by standard specialized government departments— the result is usually little more than the mere physical improvement itself, and not much is accomplished in the interests of building a more articulate and effective community life.

Another function that the USOM technicians wanted to remove was the Bongah program of instruction on the formation and management of cooperatives, although cooperatives offered the only practical means by which most villagers could own and operate modern farm machinery and engage in many other practices that would increase the economic productivity. Unless the building of a stronger economy is made a part of the process of community development in a country like Iran, community development becomes a mere whistling in the dark.

Another function to be removed from the Bongah was one devoted to involving women in the community development process in order to lift their status to something better than that of a drudge so that their potential contribution to community life could be realized. The fourth function to come out was one designed to encourage village handicrafts.

Fortunately, after long and vigorous negotiations the recommendations to remove these functions from the Bongah were not carried out, though a number of attempts were made to do so. However, the USOM gradually withdrew its financial support from the project agreements which had made these functions possible to begin with, thus adding to the Bongah's struggle to stay solvent and meet its payroll. The Iranians were finding out what Americans mean by the slogan, "You can't beat City Hall."

In 1957, the ICA decided to limit the advisory services being handled by the Near East Foundation, and in 1958 decided to get along without the Near East Foundation and hire its own employees to advise the Bongah.

By the time these advisors were hired and on the job it had been almost nine years since the United States foreign aid agency had started to build a community development program in Iran. Here because of the pressure of an emergency situation which had loomed as a threat to international peace and because of the previously established program of the Near East Foundation and a few imaginative people in the foreign aid agency itself, ICA more than in any other country in the world can be credited with the promotion of a community development program. But after nine years, the ICA became almost as great an obstruction to the program as it was in other countries whose own efforts in this field were met by subtle resistance, sometimes even open hostility, certainly never strong leadership, from the ICA.

The situation in Iran was a curious one. Here ICA sponsorship of community development was something of an accident. It got itself involved in the role of chief promoter before its own internal power structure fully realized what was happening. Later, community development in Iran became an anathema to ICA officials just as it was in other countries because of ICA's desire to control programs and operate in its traditional pattern of subject-matter specialization.

In 1958, a few months after the Bongah had trained and hired two hundred workers for the village society aspect of its work, the USOM brought enough pressure to cause these workers to be fired and to reverse the emphasis of the program to development blocks. The wisdom of this emphasis is not questioned, but the method employed to enforce the decision was such as to create deep resentment among responsible Iranians toward American officials. However, pressure, demands, orders, the presentation of USOM decisions as *fait accompli,* even tactics of ridicule which hurt Iranian pride, became the pattern of USOM dealings with the Bongah. Shouting and swearing were not uncommon, and knowledge of the situation spread through Tehran and out into the countryside. One irate Iranian expressed the feeling of many when he said, "The Americans in Point Four act like they are the landlords."

With interpersonal relationships at this level, the irritations caused by the frequent changes in USOM community development policy which were rarely explained to the Iranians, were made worse, and the Bongah suffered accordingly. But one of the underlying problems in program operations continued to be the lack of knowledge within the USOM itself of what community development actually meant.

The effects of this situation were such as to make more difficult any future effort to establish a national community development agency in Iran on an effective operating basis. At the top levels of Bongah administration there were few officials who understood the essential meaning of community development. Most Iranians who did understand it were driven out of decision-making positions in Tehran, and there was little commitment to the basic idea within the chief power echelons of the Iranian government. The Shah repeatedly spoke in favor of a more democratic society and of the needs of the great mass of the nation's population, but the powerful landlord class which controlled the government remained firm against any basic reform in the ancient social system. Thus, the Bongah itself deteriorated into just another Iranian bureaucracy in which the personal interests of government officials were considered ahead of the job to be done, and in which action was stifled by delay and indecision.

But there is ample evidence to show that effective community development by Iranians with American assistance is possible. The work of the Near East Foundation in the Varamin Plains has been one example. Another example is now being vividly demonstrated in an area called Gorgan in northern Iran next to the Russian border. There, scattered over a fertile plain between the Caspian Sea and a great range of mountains which wall off the rest of Iran to the south leaving this area exposed to the Communist giant to the north, are seven hundred villages inhabited by nearly 200,000 peasants. Their ancestors have lived there for eons. In this isolated strip of land the characteristics of all Iran are clustered into a microcosm of the nation. There in March 1958, about the same time the USOM began taking over as direct advisor to the Bongah, the Ford Foundation in cooperation with the Iranian government began a community development program independent from the USOM.

A regional office was opened, and an energetic and deeply devoted Iranian college graduate, who had trained in community development at the Varamin Rural Training Center and had three years practical experience with the Bongah, was named director. With him in the regional office was a specialist in rural construction, a specialist in public health, a specialist in women's activities, and a specialist in training. Other specialists were to be called in from the ministries as needed. An advance survey was made to collect needed information on the area, and after the program was started a community development training center was established. A young American representing the Ford Foundation and equally as energetic and devoted as the young Iranian director moved in to function as the director's helper, but with a clear understanding that the director and the other Iranian staff members were to be responsible for the program operations and were free to accept or reject any suggestion the representative of the Ford Foundation might offer.

Today they are working in four development blocks, each with a block officer trained and experienced in rural community development, and a staff of trained *dehyars* living in the villages and serving without restriction in all aspects of community life. In all there are eighty *dehyars* covering 238 villages with 98,000 people. Plans are to extend the program to cover the entire Gorgan area as rapidly as possible. *Dehyars* were sent to the Varamin Rural Training Center until the training center in Gorgan could be opened. The *dehyars* are young men with at least a sixth-grade education, and are carefully selected from the Gorgan area on the basis of intelligence, personal conviction, leadership talent, and ability to relate in a warm, personal way with villagers.

When I was in Gorgan two years after the operation began, whole villages were being renovated, new schools and health centers opened, roads constructed, improved farming methods adopted, crop yields increased, livestock vaccinated; citizens' groups were at work, and two thousand adults were learning to read and write. They had a list of 102 major activities, each representing many village achievements, that filled nine single-spaced typewritten pages.

But what I will never forget was the spirit of the whole operation—in the villages, in the relationships between the people and the *dehyars*, in the staff itself, and between the Iranians and the American agency, the Ford Foundation. In contrast to the history and relationships of the USOM and the Bongah, here a really constructive job was being done. Here was living evidence of the responsiveness of the people when properly approached.

In one of the villages a young man showed me his bandaged hand, and told me that before the *dehyar* came they used to put dirt on cuts. Here the *dehyar* was so loved by the people that when he returned from a trip on one occasion the whole village population came out to greet him. The block officer told me how the *dehyars* consulted with the people on all their life problems from marriage to farming, and how intimate they became with the village families. We went to visit the *dehyars* and watch them at work and I could see what the block officer meant. He told me the *dehyars* might work eighteen hours one day and five hours the next, depending on how much they were needed. When a *dehyar* goes out to make his rounds he leaves a note telling people where he will be in case anyone needs him. Here the *dehyar* is truly a friend of the village.

"When a boss sets regular hours for people they only work for the salary," said the block officer. "Our *dehyars* work for the people."

Gorgan is an example of a productive community development program. Here they have succeeded in creating a unified operation with all the specialized services that are needed for the development of communities. But here there is no tension between the helpers and the helped. There is no argument over definitions, no jealousy over who does what, and there is no jurisdictional dispute among specialists.

"Here," said the Iranian director, "we are improving the economy and the agriculture of this area, but in the process we are building democracy."

Perhaps the best test of those words is that in this strategic northern frontier area of Iran along the Russian border, the Iranian director himself has been pictured as an arch enemy of the people by Communist propaganda broadcasts beamed from across the border. To that he said, "I'm lucky. The *dehyars* and the people are doing the work and the Russians are giving me the credit."

I saw other examples of the great potential in Iran. I saw it in members of the Bongah who have ignored the tensions of Tehran. I saw it in the smooth and effective operations of CARE. I saw it in the remarkable work of Miss Farman-Farmaian, who spent eleven years studying and doing social work in the United States and now with help from the United Nations is overcoming tremendous obstacles to build a school to train social workers in Iran. In three years of operation this school has turned out forty graduates and is gearing itself to serve the vast slums of the Iranian capital.

One day an Iranian official called and asked me if I would accompany him on what he called a "white elephant tour"—a tour of construction projects that did not work, and which he said had been built in the "Point Four community development program." In each of half a dozen villages crowds of peasants living under some of the worst conditions of squalor I had seen came out shouting grievances against the Americans for projects they said were no good.

"But," I protested to my guide, "these people seem to just expect somebody to come along and do something for them. They show no signs of wanting to help themselves. Just building things for people is not community development."

"Well," said the official, "it *has* been in Iran."

In one village we inspected an expensive bathhouse with modern shower fixtures and stalls which had never been used. The windows had been broken and the floors were covered with several inches of top soil from the surrounding wind-blown fields. I had seen several bathhouses in this condition, and was told that there were hundreds of them.

I asked the village headman why it was like this.

"Your American engineer," said the old man, putting his hands to his ears, "was very deaf."

"He means," said the Iranian official, "that your engineer would not listen to the villagers when they told him how they wanted the bathhouse constructed. They like a Persian-type bath with a steam room and a pool. This is a shower-type bathhouse like you have in the United States, and they won't use it. It was designed to be sanitary, but no one took the

trouble to win the villagers' confidence and lead them to see
its advantages."

"You know," said my companion, "these villagers are
listening all the time to radio voices from Moscow telling
them the Americans just do enough to make things look
good, but aren't really interested in helping people. And it
is hard to teach them anything different."

Back in my hotel in Tehran I picked up one of Iran's leading dailies. In it was a report on a speech delivered on the
floor of the Majlis (the Iranian Parliament) which read,
". . . if all American government departments were managed
as were the Point Four [ICA] offices, God help Iran if it
copied the American system. . . . in such a case Iranian administration would completely disintegrate."

I threw the paper on the bed and stood in the French
doorway overlooking a Persian garden behind which rose a
range of snow-capped mountains, and I thought about the
people on the opposite side of the globe, back home in the
United States. I thought about the basic goodness, the
generosity, and the faith of a lot of people. And I thought:
If the Iranians only knew the America I know.

Then I remembered the peasants in all the mud villages
I had been in. The fact was most of them really did not have
a chance. It wasn't just that the houses they lived in weren't
any good, that they didn't have sanitation, or that they lived
in poverty. It was the system, a whole country of peasant
villages for centuries owned body and soul by landlords.
Why should they do any differently than wait for somebody
else to take care of them? And the landlords—Why should
they suddenly see things any differently?

I remembered the words of an informed young Iranian
who swore me to secrecy when he told me what life and the
government in Iran really meant, and how impossible it was
to get anything done. "You don't know what it means to live
under a dictatorship," he said. "We don't have any freedom.
Newspapers can't print a story unless it is cleared. We are
not even free to vote as we believe. Somebody, the landlord
or the government, has always told the people what to do

and what they should think. They have never learned to depend on themselves."

I thought of the size of the job to be done, and of what would be required to get it accomplished.

And then I thought of Gorgan.

8

OPPORTUNITIES ABUNDANT

ON THE MORNING OF DECEMBER 7, 1960, THE REPRESENTA-
tives of ten nations assembled at Baguio City in the
Philippines to begin the first international conference on
community development under the sponsorship of the Southeast Asia Treaty Organization. In the closing session after
nine days of talk, the American delegation expressed great
satisfaction with the conference. It made hopeful reference
to the call of the newly elected President of the United
States, John F. Kennedy, for all Americans to help take hold
of the great problems facing the world, and to the President's reminder that peoples in many parts of the world are
striking out on new courses for themselves.

"We Americans," the delegation quoted the President,
"need not be afraid of changes which arise out of hopes and
aspirations, which we, ourselves, share with other peoples in
many parts of the world." Then said the delegation in its
official statement, "Community development provides a
large common denominator of these shared hopes."

On that formal note of optimism the SEATO conference
came to a close. But the experienced delegates from the
Asian countries knew that stretching into the past was a
decade of struggle to create that "large common denominator," and that despite the idealism echoed in the conference, more years of struggle were still ahead.

149

Within less than a month after the conference ended the ICA mission in Pakistan announced that it was closing out its Division of Community Development and withdrawing support from Pakistan's national community development program. After expressions of public indignation in Karachi in which this ICA move was labeled a unilateral action, the USOM in Pakistan calmly reported that it did not regard community development as a priority program.

When Pakistan wanted to start its national program of community development ten years earlier the agricultural officials in the United States foreign aid organization had responded by trying to ease the Pakistanis into a replica of the American agricultural extension system. But the Pakistan officials with their more than 100,000 primitive villages in which over 80 per cent of the nation's estimated 88 million people lived, were not quite convinced. The United States officials then attempted to woo the Pakistanis by treating them to a special tour of agricultural extension in the United States. After months of official sales treatment the Pakistanis were impressed, but politely reported that the established American system of agricultural extension was not quite suited to the job that needed to be done in Pakistan, and further expressed their desire to organize a national program of community development.

This program was finally launched by the Pakistan government in 1953 under the official name of Village Agricultural and Industrial Development, but like other national community development programs was aimed at enriching the over-all physical and social environment of the villages. The planning board of Pakistan not only approved the program but gave it high priority in the nation's first five-year plan and re-emphasized its basic purpose by saying, "It must be kept firmly in mind that the primary objective is to develop people and their ability to help themselves. This goal must never be lost sight of as can easily happen if physical targets are made primary. The success of Village AID is assured when it places its faith in the people of the village and in their ability to think for themselves; to organize themselves for community planning and action; to use the help of government departments to supplement their own efforts; and, to increasingly solve their own problems without outside help. This is the best hope of a better life for the millions in Pakistan's villages."

In the government's second five-year plan for the period ending June 30, 1965, the community development program, having been organized in nearly 32,000 villages, was again given high priority and projected on an even larger scale sufficient to cover virtually all villages in the country. Pakistan had moved even further ahead and started community development for urban areas.

But the efforts of the ICA to twist the program into the image of United States agricultural extension never ceased. In the earlier days when it had been necessary to go along they had placated the Pakistanis by designating a few USOM agricultural extension personnel in Pakistan as "community development advisors" though still carrying these technicians on the payroll in Washington as what they actually were, agricultural advisors. Later a USOM community Development Division was formed, but gradually that was cut back until it was reduced to a one-man office, and then dropped.

When I received this report on the final action on community development by the ICA mission in Karachi after I had returned to America, I could not help but think of the words of an old man I met in a Pakistan village near Peshawar.

"Our program," he said, "is being carried on in the spirit that drove your American pioneers across your western plains during the early history of the United States."

Today national community development programs are being attempted in many countries with varying degrees of success. In no case have these programs realized their full potential. But they do represent great opportunities which in most cases are being given all too little attention.

As I moved from one part of the world to another I also discovered that in many isolated corners of the globe projects are being carried on quietly by dedicated workers with small private funds, which offer additional opportunities for community development. Most of these projects have not yet grown into the comprehensive and integrated kind of programs I would call community development. But many of these projects suggest the immense possibilities that currently exist for starting such programs, and it was in these projects that I found some of the best examples of the leadership that is needed at the operating level if these possibilities are to be turned into reality.

One of these projects (which already had become a community development program) was going on under the joint sponsorship of the Congregational Christian Service Committee and CARE in thirty villages high in the mountains of the Karpenisian area of west central Greece, the ancestral home of about thirty thousand people. Program operations centered in the village of Krikellon, which, like its neighboring villages, was built in this remote alpine terrain long ago to escape the Turks who occupied Greece for nearly four hundred years. The area was devastated by invading armies during World War II, after which the villagers rebuilt their homes only to be ravaged again during the years of guerrilla fighting through which the Communists kept Greece in a state of armed violence until 1950.

The destruction of prolonged warfare reduced the livestock herds which had long been the backbone of the area's economy to a small fraction of pre-war numbers. Severe erosion resulting from centuries of wasteful forestry had left the steep mountainsides poor and rocky and unsuited to most kinds of farming. The villagers were largely uneducated and unaware of modern agricultural techniques, and they were too poor to afford anything but scrubby stock and primitive equipment. With per capita income at $150 a year and the average farmer idle four to five months a year, economic production in the area was insufficient to provide any more than bare subsistence.

Roads in the area were closed by heavy snows a good part of each year. Many of the villages had no road at all and travel in and out could only be done by foot or on horseback up and down the steep sides of the mountains. Even when the snows had melted, the road into Krikellon, one of the principal villages in the area, was so bad that it took two hours by jeep to travel a little more than seven miles from the main highway. Health and sanitary services were virtually nonexistent, and the villagers had little hope of being able either to help themselves or of getting help to come in from the outside. They were ripe prey for the Communist infiltration which had been going on in Greece ever since the close of World War II.

Then one day the governor of Evritanias, one of the two states in which this area is located, sought help for the area from Newell Steward of the Congregational Christian Service Committee. Steward was a man in his early sixties who had been successful in the printing business, but who had devoted many years to improving the conditions of migrant laborers and rural communities in the United States, and who went to Greece with his wife in 1955 to direct operations for the Congregational Christian Service Committee. Steward was deeply interested in helping, but it took the better part of two years to find enough money to support a small staff and arrange necessary equipment. With funds raised by his own agency and by the Unitarian Church Committee of Canada, Steward obtained the services of Chris Kehayias, a Greek national who had grown into a skilled community worker while serving with Steward on another project in the ancient region of Greek Macedonia.

Chris was exactly the man Steward needed. He was a graduate of the American Farm School at Salonica, established by an American missionary to teach practical agriculture and Christian leadership; both these objectives had taken firm root in Chris Kehayias' mind. After working as a farm manager he had spent three years fighting Communist guerrillas.

"I hated the Communists," Chris told me. "I saw how cruel men can be. But I couldn't hate the common people who collaborated with them because many were forced, and poverty in Greece was so bad that many felt there was no other way. Many still feel that way today. But little by little I learned that the only hope for Greece in the long run is for some kind of program to help our depressed people forget the past and gain new hope for a better life by peaceful means. That is why I wanted Mr. Steward to transfer into my mind his ideas of community development. That is what I intend to do with my life from now on."

Fighting their way through snowdrifts and traveling by jeep and by foot over roads that were just barely passable, Steward and Chris made several trips into the villages of the Krikellon area to begin getting acquainted and map out a plan of operations. Going from village to village they struck up conversations with anyone they met until they were able to identify the recognized village leaders, and had a good idea of what would be of most interest to the people. Late in 1957, Chris began living most of each week in the area and made a systematic survey to further pinpoint the village leaders and determine what the people themselves felt was most needed. While Steward was busy arranging for the necessary staff and equipment, Chris moved forward in Krikellon generating interest among the villagers and laying the foundations for calling the first meeting and the actual launching of a community development program.

Finally, when he felt the mood of the villagers was right, Chris went to the village leaders and set a time and place to begin. The first meeting was held in Krikellon in January 1958 with twenty-seven men in attendance. Chris and Steward were both there. Chris opened the meeting, reviewed the assets and liabilities of the village, and mentioned possible improvements that could be made to get rid of the liabilities. As he talked he gave particular emphasis to the problems the leaders had already discussed with him in individual conversations during his advance study, and he described the idea of a community development program and how it would operate (which he had also discussed with them individually before the meeting). Steward told them about the Congregational Christian Service Committee and said they would be willing to work with the villagers if the villagers decided they wanted to go ahead. Both he and Chris made it clear that nothing could be accomplished, that in fact they would not even be interested in helping, unless the villagers were willing to work and organize a village development group to be responsible for planning and carrying out a work program. Then they left the villagers alone to decide for themselves whether or not they wanted to assume this responsibility. The decision was never in doubt. Chris had done his advance job thoroughly and enough interest had already been generated to get started even before the meeting was held.

When I arrived in Krikellon in 1960, development committees had been organized and were at work in twenty-one of the thirty villages with the other nine scheduled to come in shortly; from these groups an organization had been formed to represent the entire area. In the area organization they had an elected executive committee and a series of special action committees for each of the various work projects which were going forward on an areawide basis. Each village organization was concentrating on problems peculiar to that village, while the area organization worked on problems of common concern to all the villages and supplied an additional stimulus for the village committees.

Meanwhile, Steward had sought joint sponsorship for the program from CARE, which responded with $15,000-worth of aid from private American donors to help provide the materials and supplies that were needed. Without CARE's entry into the effort, the Krikellon program could never have moved forward as it did, for the people in this remote mountainous area could not have mustered from their own resources enough capital to make the difference that was needed in their basic economy. But the material aid would have meant nothing without the spiritual stimulation and skillful leadership supplied by Steward and his associates, and the internal community development organization through which the people gained the confidence, the determination, and the ability to help themselves. Thus, the necessary ingredients for a successful program were carefully created and assembled by a corps of dedicated workers and synthesized in the proper combination.

Within the framework of comprehensive village and area improvement fostered by the community development concept, a general mood for uplifting all aspects of life was carefully generated among the villagers, and within the context of this broad perspective they began to select specific projects in a variety of fields that would contribute toward their over-all goal: a better and more prosperous community in which to live. They included such fields as economic growth, transportation, education, health, homemaking, recreation, civic consciousness, advancement in the status of women, enrichment of interpersonal relationships among the people, and many other aspects of living that go into the make-up of good communities.

Their first project was, as Steward put it, "to increase the production of food for both man and beast." In the mountains there was plenty of water, but irrigation was necessary to put it where it was needed at the times it was needed. This was accomplished by cementing miles of irrigation ditches from which 75 per cent of their irrigation water was being lost through seepage. Many more ditches were dug. Two large ponds were constructed, and in some places drainage lines were installed. Tools, cement, and pipe were supplied by CARE; sand, gravel, and labor were supplied by the villagers. This action alone more than doubled alfalfa production and enabled the villagers to grow other crops that had not previously been possible.

In the area there were large numbers of fruit trees, but because the farmers knew nothing about spraying and pruning, the trees had never produced much fruit. And so spraying and pruning teams were organized, and the men in the first teams went from village to village teaching others and organizing more teams. In 1959 more spray was used in the Krikellon area than had ever been used in the entire state of Evritanias.

With CARE aid, Krikellon village was turned into a livestock breeding center for the entire area, and breeding sub-stations were set up at strategic points dotted through the mountains. For this purpose a model livestock barn was constructed at Krikellon with specialized out-buildings, a large fenced enclosure for heavily fertilized pasturage, watering tanks, pipelines, storage areas, and other facilities needed to produce the finest specimens of sheep, cattle, goats, hogs, rabbits, chickens, and bees. CARE supplied the basic breeding stock to get the center started, and Steward and Chris arranged for special training for the farmers in modern methods of livestock production.

The villagers obtained assistance from the government for the construction of a good road into Krikellon, and with a tractor and bulldozer donated by private citizens in America through CARE, the villagers began construction of branch roads, and organized work crews to maintain the roads and keep them open during the winter. With this the area was linked to the outside world by daily bus service into Krikellon.

In an area where each family raises the grain for its own flour but which had never had the right seed to produce really suitable grain, the people were made aware of what had been lacking by CARE donations of high quality seed; within two years the farmers had started making direct ar-rangements with the government agricultural bank for their own seed supplies.

When I visited the area with Steward and Larry Delli-quadri, of CARE, some of the farmers had made their first cash sales from their increased agricultural production, and scores of villagers wanted me to take pictures of their fine new calves, sheep, hogs, goats, their purebred New Hamp-shire red laying hens, and their New Zealand giant rabbits. They had a marketing committee organized to increase sales efficiency, and to explore the advisability of starting a co-operative.

With the aid of CARE materials the villagers had built a model community center in Krikellon equipped as a health station and for all-round community activities. CARE had supplied sewing machines and knitting machines, equipment for the canning of fruits, vegetables, and meat, and various other equipment for recreation and adult education purposes. People were coming in from the surrounding villages to use this center, and from the incentive it provided, five other villages had built community centers of their own, two more were scheduled to be completed within the next sixty days, and as rapidly as possible the area development group had decided to push for community centers in every village in the area. To supplement the centers Steward had arranged for a donkey library to go from village to village and maintain a steady supply of reading material.

The men had been busy building village parks and benches. New public wash houses with hot and cold water and new sanitary public toilets had been installed. They had been laying pipe for sanitary sewer systems, and in one village where women had been carrying water up the mountainside for thousands of years, the villagers had installed piped running water.

Chris had set up staff headquarters in a two-story stone house in Domnista, a village just across the mountain from Krikellon and connected by a new road which the villagers had recently finished. The staff house, in which I stayed overnight, was a plain building with a fairly large room on the second floor used as combination living and dining quarters, a small kitchen, and bedrooms for the staff. It had no heat except the little bit that came from a small stove in the common room, and in the bedroom I occupied there was a fireplace.

To help Chris carry on the program operations Steward had obtained the services of three young women from Athens who had been trained in social work and who had eagerly accepted this opportunity to learn community development. He had hired a man to work full time at the livestock center in Krikellon, and through the state government he had arranged for two home economists and an agricultural technician to conduct classes and provide specialized advice. Once the over-all program had been established

Steward and his associates continuously emphasized the value to the villagers of using outside specialists in the various aspects of the program, and at one of the area meetings they brought in representatives from sixteen government agencies and two private cooperatives to explain the services they were prepared to offer. It was Steward's belief that one of the important elements in community development was teaching the people when and how to make use of technicians in the various specialized fields.

Operations of the program imposed a rigorous and demanding life upon Chris and the three girls who made up the staff. Each day, seven days a week, they were up for an early morning breakfast, usually consisting of thick dark brown Turkish coffee, milk, bread, and hard boiled eggs. Taking turns, one of the girls was in charge of the housework for the day, did the cooking, and greeted the numerous villagers who came in to talk over problems, or just to talk. The staff headquarters had become something of a community center in itself. The other girls were responsible for attending scheduled meetings, calling on families individually, and conducting special classes for teenagers out of school, three days a week for boys, and two days a week for girls. On Saturdays they held planned recreational and educational activities for younger children.

From their headquarters at Domnista, Chris and his young staff members traveled by horseback making their rounds of the villages, conducting classes, holding meetings, counseling with the people, lending encouragement to their efforts, suggesting new ideas, and helping in the organization of action projects. Each day those who had travels to make would start out over the mountain trails soon after breakfast, and not get back until ten or eleven o'clock at night. Often they went out for one to two weeks at a time, sometimes staying several days to a week or more in one village, depending upon the projects they had under way. A good community development worker must be able to create opportunities for citizen action and know how and to what extent to move in when opportunities arise. In the winter, deep snows and heavy drifts made travel slow and difficult, and all members of the staff adhered strictly to the rule not to travel when there was danger of a snowstorm.

I had a long talk with one of the young women members of the staff, a striking girl in her twenties named Eleni Ougoungeorgie who would have been as much at home in a fashionable dining room in Athens as she was working with the peasants in these remote mountain villages. She was a tall, attractive brunette, as dedicated to the welfare of Greece as Chris himself. She had experienced the suffering of living under Nazi occupation, and during the Greek guerrilla wars she had been in the thick of the fighting which went on in one of the areas near Athens.

She described how they had been able to help the villagers make a beginning toward elevating the status of women. For hundreds of years tradition and custom in rural Greece have held women to a life of drudgery and, in effect, second class citizenship. Only as recently as 1953 have women in Greece been allowed to vote, but this has had little effect on the substandard position of women in the rural areas where about two-thirds of the people live. In areas such as that around Krikellon the prescribed role of the woman has been to do her work and stay out of public places as much as possible. By established custom she labors in the fields, frequently while her husband loafs around the village coffee house, cares for the children, tends to the animals, carries water, builds the morning fires, and does as her husband tells her. It has been considered improper for her to attend meetings, even with other women, and she has had no voice in village affairs. Education for girls has been considered unimportant, and when a family has not had enough food or money to go around it has been tradition for the women and girls to get whatever is left after the men and boys are cared for. Parties and social events have been chiefly for men only.

In the cities of Greece today this ancient custom is no longer standard practice, and because of the work of Eleni and her associates, definite alterations in the system were being made even in the isolated mountainous villages of the Krikellon area. Gradually, they were getting groups of women organized for meetings in the community centers, and some of the men told me they would be happy to have women serve on the village development committees. These changes in the basic social system were virtually revolutionary in this part of Greece. In these women's meetings, mothers were studying the principles of nutrition and other essentials of good homemaking. They had set up community canning centers and were learning modern methods of food preservation.

Another move was the organization in each of the villages of special groups of young women for recreational and educational purposes. Even a year earlier this would have been unthinkable because the fathers would never have permitted it. But this move had advanced to such a point that the girls had started visiting from village to village to exchange ideas, and had even suggested a trip to Athens to visit museums and other places in the city to broaden their education. It would perhaps be a little difficult for most Western women to appreciate the significance of this aspect of developing democracy in community life, but in the social setting in this part of Greece this was one of the most far-reaching changes to grow out of the entire program. If this change continues, the day may come when the women of this area will be freed of the ancient social restraints which for generations have prevented them from making their full contribution to the enrichment of family and community life.

The gradual development of democracy along with the development of the economy was one of the most exhilarating things I had seen. I found that it had not yet been possible to hold general village meetings in which the whole population could participate, but they were working toward that. One important step in this direction was the starting of an annual community fair for all villagers in the area. Here the people could display their livestock, canned goods, and handwork made in the recreation workshops in the community centers. Other steps toward total citizen participation were mass action projects, such as when virtually an entire village turned out for the laying of a pipe line. Meanwhile the village and area development committees are growing in importance and prestige, and as one man put it, "We always have eager workers on our committees because if they aren't eager we replace them."

At the community centers the school teachers were helping with classes for adults and young people. In Domnista the teacher told me this was making it possible to reach many people who could not be reached any other way. He said many people had left elementary school years before when standards were very low and that now as part of their community development program they were coming back to study reading and writing, arithmetic, geography, and history.

"And," he said, "people are learning to read the newspaper, and they are learning that the Communists can't give us the solution to our problems."

The captain of the police said, "Community development is improving the civilization of our villages. People go to the community center to see plays by our young people. They sit and play table games, and they read books. These things never happened before."

Another man said, "The community development program is a big school and through that school must pass all our people."

I asked a farmer why he had walked ten miles across the mountains to attend an area meeting in Domnista, and he said, "I would walk ten miles every day for this because we are rebuilding our lives."

For two days I walked through the villages, talking to the people, hearing their optimism which they told me had not existed before. I visited in their homes, sat in their coffee houses and drank Turkish coffee. I met with them in small groups and large groups. We ate together and sang songs together, and we toasted the future of Greece. I inspected their projects and saw the physical evidence of their efforts, but I felt and heard something much more important than that. The mayor put it this way, "We have here a new spirit and it is growing up. We are developing spiritual and material values together."

As we drove away from the high mountains and villages of Krikellon, a crowd of villagers stood to wave goodbye. Suddenly the church bells began ringing and I felt what the people had told me they felt. In this village Greeks and Americans had truly become partners in a common cause.

Krikellon is an example of a community development program conducted with limited resources when it is led by dedicated workers who are willing to learn its basic meaning and who have the personal skills to put it into operation. For those who know the practice of community development and who have the vision to see its power for the strengthening of democracy, the world is full of opportunities.

I visited many projects that were not community development programs as was Krikellon, but in which excellent work was being done and which contained some of the essential ingredients of community development. Projects such as these being carried on all over the non-Communist world give a clear indication of some of the possible ways by which community development programs could be started if sufficient support and properly trained or experienced community development leaders were made available.

In South Vietnam the project of Hung Phuoc, which translated literally means Lucky Village, illustrates this opportunity. It was started as the result of action taken by a group of refugees known as the Nungs who had lived in a section along the border between China and North Vietnam and who had come into South Vietnam in search of a chance for freedom. During the violent struggles with Communist forces and the religious sects following the establishment of North and South Vietnam in 1954 they had fought vigorously for President Diem, but by 1958 had still been unable to find a stable livelihood.

Finally, under the leadership of a determined man named Watson Lau, a party of about twenty-five of them had pushed off in boats up the Dong Nai River into wild, uninhabited jungle country, and at a point along the river about fifty miles from Saigon had cut out a small area in the jungle just large enough to make camp. On the first night their camp was stampeded by wild elephants. The next day sixteen members of the party quit the expedition and returned to Saigon. The remaining nine, pressed by Watson's encouragement, were working from dawn to dusk with nothing but a few ancient hand tools trying to cut through the tough, tangled mat of jungle vegetation to clear a large enough area to plant crops and build a new community.

Watson had tried everywhere to get help but without success, until he met Harold Sillcox, chief of the CARE mission to South Vietnam. After visiting the camp and analyzing the possibilities, Sillcox supplied enough food and tools for immediate needs, and obtained authorization from CARE's New York headquarters to help build the new community, which Watson Lau and his followers decided to call Hung Phuoc, or Lucky Village.

As more people moved up the river the cleared area became larger, and they erected a bunk house to afford greater protection from the jungle. Day after day they worked in driving monsoon rains. They were pestered by swarms of insects, and during one period half the members of the settlement were stricken by malaria. The jungle was full of leeches that crawled over their skin and sucked blood from their bodies. There were irritating plants and thorns that caused swelling and itching. There were deadly snakes, including cobras and pythons, and there were elephants, tigers, and panthers. At night they were kept awake by the noise of marauding jungle beasts. But Watson Lau and his people were determined to make the project succeed, and CARE continued to supply enough aid to keep it moving. One of their most difficult achievements was the building of a road nearly three miles through the jungle to connect with an established road so that supplies, equipment, and people could move into the area when the swift river currents became too swollen by the rains to permit travel by boat.

Two years later in 1960, I went with Harold Sillcox to

visit Hung Phuoc. Over three hundred acres of land had been cleared and eighty families consisting of about four hundred people had moved into the settlement. Each family was farming its own plot of land and living in its own house. As new families moved in they were given a plot of ground and the settlers already there helped them build a home and get started.

CARE, which had been their only outside source of aid, had supplied equipment such as a caterpillar tractor, a bulldozer blade, a disk harrow, a tree hog, a generator, several engines, and a block-making machine for building construction. Other equipment supplied by American donors through CARE included axes, picks, shovels, crosscut saws, and other hand tools, blankets, medicines, and mosquito nets.

With pumps supplied by CARE they had installed an irrigation system for use during the dry season. A rice and starch mill was being installed to process raw products from the fields into commodities for marketing, and a community center had been constructed where the women produced clothing for their families with CARE sewing machines. They had organized a variety of activities for the children with CARE recreational equipment; the settlers were in the process of building a school; an effort was being made to locate a teacher.

Three babies had been born in the settlement, and a small health center had been established with Watson dispensing emergency treatment. In two years he had distributed more than five thousand quinine pills to help fight malaria, and no one knows how many aspirin tablets, bandages, and other first aid items. For treatment of major illness their only alternative was to move the patient into Saigon.

The new community had suffered many setbacks. On one occasion a fungus blew in from the jungle and destroyed most of the crops. But despite all obstacles the settlement was rapidly reaching the point of self-sufficiency, and several merchants were planning to establish retail shops. In the planning of CARE aid Harold Sillcox had worked closely with Watson and the people to make certain that this help would stimulate the continued growth of self-reliance and a spirit of cooperation within the settlement. Each piece of equipment was delivered as a part of a plan democratically charted by the people with the guidance of Watson and Sillcox, and based upon the people's labor and achievements. The results of this kind of planning were plain to see.

Under Watson's guidance the people had formed themselves into a community organization to manage their common affairs and to plan and develop the social as well as the physical aspects of community life. When I was there they were having a religious feast in which it was customary practice for only the men to participate. But Watson had said that such customs retarded progress because they set up a double standard between men and women, and that in their new community, customs of this kind should be dropped.

In a meeting with the men at which this issue was vigorously discussed, Watson was accused of wanting this change only because he was a bachelor and therefore did not understand women. Watson argued that the women worked hard in building the community, and that everyone who worked deserved to take part in the feast. But, the men argued, if women took part it would anger the gods. Watson countered this objection by asking what the female gods might think, and finally persuaded the men. Then the women held back on the grounds that they had to work and take care of the children.

"I told them to forget their work for a while and bring the children with them," said Watson. "Now the whole community is having fun working together and making decisions together. This is what we must do to make democracy."

Watson Lau was an amazing individual. He was about forty, had come from a prominent Chinese family, but pointed out that he and all the others in the new community had become citizens of South Vietnam. He was well-educated, spoke good English, possessed considerable experience in organization and business management, and was a leader with strong feelings for the welfare of the community which

he had led into being. He had become what amounted to a
volunteer community development worker, for which he possessed obvious personal talent.

I asked him why he was doing all this when there were
so many other things he could do that would be so much
more profitable to him personally.

"When my father laid down," he said, "he called me to
his side and told me he wanted me to work hard and look
after our people, and this is what I must do."

I had met people like Watson in many countries, but I
could not help but think how important it is to have people
like Sillcox employed by organizations like CARE to search
them out, work with them, encourage them, and help them
on the person-to-person basis I saw here in this remote
pioneer settlement in the jungle wilds of Southeast Asia.

There are few countries in the world that have illustrated
more dramatically than South Vietnam the need for a national program of community development. Ever since the
Geneva Conference of 1954 which carved this country out
of what was formerly French Indo-China, South Vietnam
has been subjected to the pressure of Communist guerrilla
forces from the North known as the Viet Cong. Through
the years these forces grew in strength and offensive action
until by 1961 South Vietnam had become a major focal point
of the Communist thrust into Southeast Asia, thousands of
people were being slaughtered, the American-backed government of Ngo Dinh Diem was in serious trouble, and in
spite of the hundreds of millions of dollars in United States
military and economic aid that had been poured into the
country, the hope for world peace had been darkened by
the threat of another Communist takeover.

One of the basic factors that made it possible for this
situation to develop was that the mass of the people in South
Vietnam felt little confidence or respect for their own government, and as a consequence had little if any desire to
defend it. In the rural areas the people lived by night under
the threat of the Viet Cong, by day under the coercive
methods of the government of Ngo Dinh Diem; from the

standpoint of their own welfare they could make little distinction between the two. The majority of the contacts the people experienced with their own government were oppressive and authoritarian in nature. Other than this, the legal government had little meaning in the rural areas where most of the population lived, and it was this gap between government and people that largely made it possible for the guerrilla operations of the Viet Cong to be carried on with so high a degree of success.

Had an operation based on the principles of community development, such as I saw in Lucky Village, been carried out on a nationwide scale under government sponsorship through the years beginning with the birth of the republic in 1954, the success of the guerrilla tactics of the Viet Cong would have been significantly reduced. There was in South Vietnam during these years a national department of civic action employing several thousand field agents in an operation often referred to as community development, but that was a serious misnomer. Civic action was in effect an oppressive device used by the government to tell the people what to think and do; it aroused widespread animosity.

In a true program of community development operating on a nationwide scale such as that in the Philippines, the thousands of field agents employed by civic action could have been used to build viable citizens' organizations in villages throughout the country to engage in constructive activities such as were carried on in Lucky Village. In this kind of an operation the civic action field agents could have provided a connecting link with the people that would have enabled the Diem administration to make itself favorably felt in the daily life of the population. It could have built up a nationwide relationship of mutual trust and cooperation between government and people that would have acted as a powerful deterrent to the guerrilla invasion from North Vietnam. Community development could thus have become a powerful weapon in the military defense of South Vietnam while at the same time building the intangible human and social quality that is essential to the growth of democracy.

It is this quality, call it civic responsibility or call it what you may, that constitutes one of the basic ingredients of community development. Once that quality is brought to life as I witnessed it in Lucky Village, then people can be counted upon to take care of themselves insofar as they are physically able, and to respond intelligently and effectively when outside aid is offered—either for the defense of their national integrity or for the improvement of their standard of living. Without that quality there is little likelihood that the less developed areas of the world can ever be helped to overcome their present miserable conditions by democratic means, regardless of how much money is spent to help them.

On a barren stretch of land along the western coast of South Korea eight hundred men, women, and children were facing starvation when they were discovered by George D. Taylor, chief of the CARE mission to South Korea. Supplies of CARE food kept them alive, and under Taylor's guidance they organized a self-help effort which has made this one of the proudest villages I saw in the Orient. After months of toil they moved tons of earth from the tidelands of the Yellow Sea and constructed a salt works to provide themselves with a means of earning a living, and they reclaimed land on which to grow enough crops to feed themselves. In addition to the food that was required to get the project started, CARE supplied a little over $2,000-worth of tools and equipment, and with that small investment this village became self-sufficient.

The obvious appreciation of the people and their admiration for George Taylor were more than gratifying. But what was even more gratifying was the spirit expressed by the village leader.

"Now we can earn our own living," he said, "and we are very happy."

I saw this spirit of self-help in the work of CARE in Turkey, Israel, Iran, Pakistan, Ceylon, Haiti, Panama, Costa Rica, and Honduras. I saw it when I accompanied Fred Davis, a CARE representative in India, on one of his periodic visits to Dalhousie at the foot of the Himalayas where Gyalo Thondup, sister-in-law of the Dalai Lama, is leading the development of a new community for Tibetan refugees. CARE has been able to cultivate these projects because in the countries where it is working it has made a point to search out people who are attempting to foster them. Virtually all of these projects present opportunity for community development.

Mary Elmendorf, a vivacious South Carolinian, who was chief of the CARE mission to Mexico when I was there in 1960, had ferreted out people all over the country, both inside and outside the Mexican government, who were carrying on programs with community development possibilities, and she was pushing all of them. By her own personality and because of the way she worked with people, she had become one of the best known and best liked women in Mexico. To thousands of villagers throughout the country she was known as "Señora Care."

One of her favorite persons was an energetic Mexican woman, Alicia Godoy Ramirez, director of rural improvement for the Department of Agriculture in the state of Mexico which surrounds the capital city. Mexico City is one of the most modern cities in Latin America, but within a few miles of its boundaries the country fades into a vast plateau of adobe villages. Here people live in poverty and ignorance. For most of them life is little different today from what it was five hundred years ago. In her capacity with the state government, Alicia Godoy had organized and trained ninety-four young women into a corps of village workers to help change these conditions. When I was there, Alicia Godoy and her girl village workers were operating in 114 villages, and with CARE equipment and Mary El-mendorf's personal encouragement were beginning to effect a transformation in the life of the villages.

Alicia Godoy worked on the thesis that the best way into the village was through the family, and that because women represented a cornerstone of family life they would be her point of contact. It was her conviction that the traditional position of women in village society had amounted to a form of slavery, and that once this was changed a volatile new force for a better community life would be created. And based on the results she and her corps of girls were getting there could be little argument with her assumptions.

Over a period of time it had become noticeable in the villages that the women were considerably better educated and more competent in knowing how to handle village problems than the men, and this was becoming a powerful stimulant for improvement among the men. Gradually the women had taken on a new position of importance in village life, and because of the abilities displayed by the girl village workers the mayors and village elders were beginning to look to them for advice and counsel. It had even reached the point where men were taking off their hats when they entered a room in which there were women, and if they forgot, the village worker reminded them. In one village the men complained that since the village worker had taught the girls to play volley ball she should teach the boys to play soccer. Actually, it was adding up to a minor social revolution. And the results were better people and better villages.

Homes were being improved as the women began applying what they had learned about cooking, homemaking, and child care. Open hearth fireplaces were being raised so the women would not have to kneel on the bare earth floor to cook. In some homes kitchen cook stoves had been installed. Furniture making had become a major village activity and homes that never had even a chair or a bed were beginning to look like homes. Sanitary toilets were being installed. Compost pits for garbage disposal and fertilizer were being dug, and livestock was being kept outside or in buildings especially constructed for animals. Drainage was being installed to carry off village waste, sanitary bathing facilities were being erected, and laundry facilities were being planned so the women would not have to wash clothes in the river. Community centers had been built in which the women and girls were making new clothes, and in which adult education and village recreation were going on. New schools were being built. People were growing gardens and learning how to raise better chickens, pigs, and cows. Increased care was being taken to avoid food contamination and they were spraying to get rid of insects. They were doing these things with tools, block-making machines, sewing machines, recreational goods, school kits, books, and a long list of other supplies and equipment that had been sent by American donors through CARE.

Mary Elmendorf, Alicia Godoy, and I drove out from Toluca early one morning to watch the girl village workers and the people in action. In the little village of Santa Maria the people were almost wild with excitement over a new sanitary water well that had only recently been completed by a drilling team of young men from the United States working as volunteers with the American Friends Service Committee, under the technical supervision of Mexico's Department of Hydraulic Resources.

This team, using a drilling rig purchased by CARE for $10,000, was working a schedule designed to drill wells in all of Alicia Godoy's 114 villages, thus bringing the people of this area their first sanitary drinking water. It was estimated that up to 70 per cent of the people in these villages were suffering from infections caused by contaminated water. In Mexico as a whole it has been estimated that bad water accounts for 21 per cent of the nation's deaths.

To be eligible for a well a village had to have the equivalent of $320 on deposit in a bank to cover the cost of casing, sealing, and capping for permanent operation, and guarantee to use it only for drinking water. This money, which was a substantial amount for these particular villages, was raised by all sorts of activities and in itself represented a considerable achievement. In one village the local priest donated all the funds he had saved for remodeling the church, and in another the school children had raised half the amount needed from the sale of vegetables from their school garden plots which the village worker had taught them to grow.

The people in Santa Maria had so many achievements to show that we could hardly move fast enough from one to the other. The women through whom the new progress had been started had named their organization the Ohio Club in honor of the Ohio Federation of Women's Clubs in the United States which had been CARE's principal donor for this village.

Just as we were about to leave Santa Maria a large white truck about the size of a moving van arrived carrying three nurses in white starched uniforms, and the entire village rushed out to meet it. The CARE mobile health unit had arrived on its first scheduled run into this village. The people had been expecting it for some weeks and they actually jumped up and down and started hugging and kissing each other.

This particular unit was donated by Johnson's Wax, Procter & Gamble, the Mutual Service Life Insurance Company, and more than forty smaller United States firms. The APEI, Mexico's affiliate of the Business Council for International Understanding, had arranged to keep the health unit supplied with pharmaceutical products, hypodermic needles, and audio-visual training aids. The unit was designed to serve as a health center for communities and schools, as an emergency hospital, and as a field laboratory and health education unit. It was literally a clinic on wheels. Responsibility for professional services had been assumed by the Ministry of Health and Public Welfare.

All the material assistance being brought into this area by CARE, including the mobile health unit and the well drilling rig, Mary Elmendorf and Alicia Godoy had carefully planned to stimulate the self-help spirit of the villages. In one place, a supply of CARE books was used to stimulate the people to build their first school because the adults could not read and they wanted their children to have the benefits of using the books. Everywhere we went the villagers dropped what they were doing to show us their accomplishments and to shout, *"Viva CARE! Viva Norte Americano!"*

Basically, CARE is not a community development organization, yet it has become an important international force in the promotion and spread of the community devel-

opment concept. From its early mission of delivering packages to Europe following the destruction of World War
II, CARE expanded its operations into underdeveloped
countries around the world. With this expansion it became
increasingly evident that although relief feeding was essential to keep people alive, just keeping them alive was not
enough if societies were to be constructed in which foreign
aid would no longer be needed. Thus, a new emphasis was
placed upon the distribution of tools and equipment by
which people could help themselves, and with this emphasis
CARE began to search out projects that could be built into
programs of community development.

This interest gained rapid momentum because the men
and women in CARE, including Richard W. Reuter, its
executive director, and other top officials such as E. Gordon
Alderfer, who was a leading early proponent of the self-help
emphasis, appreciated the fact that programs of community
development, well organized and operated, meant a more
effective use of the donor dollars for which CARE was
responsible.

CARE also recognized that with careful planning its
food and materials could be distributed in such a way as to
make them an effective device for exploiting the abundant
opportunities which exist throughout the underdeveloped
world for projects that can lead to community development
and the vital experience in democracy which these projects
can provide. Because the leaders of this organization, from
its New York headquarters to its more than thirty missions
overseas, have had the vision to recognize these opportunities, CARE is today providing a channel through which
millions of Americans are sending not only packages of
food to a hungry world, but are helping to encourage
community development operations in which people in
remote places around the globe are learning self-reliance
and gaining new hope for the future.

CARE has become a significant example of how community development may be fostered and encouraged by limited
financial means through American private initiative. That

initiative, with its traditional drive, its flexibility, its freedom of action, its power of imagination, and its capacity to move effectively in the promotion of ideas and the rendering of service, has an essential role to play in the launching of the community development programs which must occupy a central place in America's response to the problems of the underdeveloped world if foreign aid is to achieve its purpose. It has been said that democracy is not applicable in all countries. But if American private initiative and official United States foreign aid could be coupled together in a worldwide community development movement aimed at building civic institutions such as have been started in Krikellon, in Lucky Village, or in Santa Maria, America would find that democracy can speak in many tongues.

9
CONCLUSIONS

POTENTIALLY, COMMUNITY DEVELOPMENT IS A POWERFUL means of creating the conditions that are essential to the growth of freedom in the newly developing countries of today's world. It is a practical and effective way to achieve a viable political, social, and economic order in Latin America, Africa, the Middle East, and the vast reaches of Asia in accordance with the principles of human dignity and self-determination. It is democracy's most positive alternative to communism. But until the meaning of community development is more widely understood in the United States, the nation that holds the chief position of power and leadership in the free world, and until it is made an integral part of American foreign aid policy, its potential will remain little more than a dream of something that ought to be. Until this concept of development is vigorously supported and promoted by the United States, the political instability, the turmoil, the social tensions, and the human miseries that contribute to the advance of world communism will continue to multiply, and the forces of democracy will be gradually eaten away.

Nothing that has been introduced in the current world struggle for progress has so typified the American pioneer tradition of work, self-help, and civic cooperation as the community development movement. And yet in all its expenditures for foreign aid the United States has given no more than token support to community development and in many cases has openly resisted it. Probably the majority of American foreign aid officials and technicians have been unaware of the concept. Many, particularly those engaged in technical assistance, have seen it as a threat to their own professional and bureaucratic interests. Others have gone along, but the few who have offered support have found it necessary not to go too far.

Many people in the United States and in other parts of the world have found this attitude difficult to comprehend. However, in light of one of the major aspects of the cultural pattern of modern America this lack of support for community development from foreign aid is quite understandable. In modern America great stress is placed upon technology and specialization. In this age it is normal and customary for Americans to think in terms of various specialized fields of knowledge that have become established in this country, such as economics, education, public health, transportation, agriculture, engineering, anthropology, social work. Each of these fields is in turn broken down into many finer specializations, and in hundreds of institutions of higher learning it is possible for a person to devote a lifetime to becoming an authority on a minute particle of human knowledge.

Around each specialization, university departments, private businesses, government agencies, and individual careers are organized, and one of the chief criteria of social prestige is the financial or professional success a person attains in one of these accepted fields of specialization. A person may contribute virtually nothing as a citizen in terms of community responsibility, but still be highly respected by his neighbors because he is successful in an established specialty. This emphasis on specialization has contributed heavily toward the advance of the American economy. But it has also made it normal for Americans, particularly highly educated Americans, to think of the problems of a country not in terms of the environment out of which the problems arise, but in terms of one of the recognized fields of specialized knowledge into which American scholars have divided and classified life.

It is therefore natural for American professionals to think not of the community in itself as constituting a problem, but rather to look upon any problem as economic, sociological, or as being in some other specialized field. Inasmuch as community development is not concerned with any specialized field but is concerned with the community as a whole, the development of which calls for a broad general approach cutting across many fields, community development becomes a concept which is difficult for the American foreign aid bureaucrat or technician to comprehend. He can think only in terms of his specialization, as a technician or a money lender. Moreover, the bureaucracy in which he is employed thinks that way too. Thus, the community development concept represents a way of dealing with problems that is strange and unnatural for him.

When the President of the United States or his top advisors or members of Congress say that America is going to share her storehouse of knowledge with the newly developing countries of the world, the agriculturist immediately and almost automatically translates that into manure piles, compost pits, and irrigation ditches. The home economist translates it into nutrition and child care. The educator translates it into school buildings and blackboards. The public health doctor translates it into latrines, mosquito abatement, and water wells. The engineer translates it into roads and public works. And other technicians translate it into projects in each of their respective fields. Almost nobody translates it into the creation of unified, active, responsible, civic-minded, problem-solving communities.

The specialists then proceed to build up divisions, sections, and budgets around each of the splinter translations they have made, and go out to start work on their respective projects as separately and independently from each other as possible so that their particular projects will stand out. Each set of projects is designed to improve something which is viewed as imperative to the future of newly developing countries in accordance with the professional values of the specialized field into which the projects fall. Those projects that are eventually judged to be the most important (and which consequently get the most money) depend largely upon which division or section of the bureaucracy has been able to marshall the most pressure.

This pattern of technical assistance in the United States foreign aid program has been exported wholesale to scores of newly developing countries throughout the world. From Latin America through Africa, the Middle East, and Asia, American technicians have aligned themselves with host country ministries that fit into their respective fields of specialization and have helped nudge them into the same pattern of conflict that has characterized the array of specialized offices and divisions within the foreign aid agency in Washington, thus adding to the inter-agency jealousies to which virtually all newly developing countries are easily susceptible.

But the exportation of this system of developing assorted specialized projects, usually unrelated to each other or to the comprehensive development of societies and communities, has not been left solely to the individual foreign aid technicians. These carriers of the system have been greatly reinforced by veritable boatloads of foreign nationals who have been brought to the United States, put through university courses in the same system, and then sent home to join forces with their American counterparts. In some countries there are now local officials who worship this splinter system of development with even greater fervor than the Americans. In some countries there is a tendency to be insulted if United States foreign aid sends over an American technician who is not sufficiently specialized to have a Ph.D.

In the face of this build-up which has been going on for more than a decade and which has enjoyed billions of dollars worth of support, it should not be surprising to find that when someone suggests an approach such as community development, he is in trouble. He is attempting to change the system. He wants to make use of the various specialists within the framework of a unified effort to strengthen the ability of whole communities of people to advance through self-determining action, with the agencies of their government joining them in the same unified manner.

This lack of American understanding of the meaning and potential of community development has been largely responsible for the failure of American foreign aid to yield a return in world political stability and human progress commensurate to the generosity of the American people, to win greater friendship from the nations receiving the aid, and to contribute more effectively toward the creation of conditions that would stem the worldwide onslaught of Sino-Soviet aggression.

Today many changes are being made in the foreign aid program of the United States. The ICA has been absorbed by the Agency for International Development. But unless the concept of community development is built into the core of foreign aid planning, and aggressively supported around the world, American aid will still be minus an essential instrument. Thus far nothing has been done by the new foreign aid agency to indicate that this action is about to be taken.

To appreciate adequately why it is so urgent that community development be made a central part of American aid to the emergent countries, it is necessary to appreciate the fact that although the standard of living in these countries is such that hunger, poverty, disease, and human suffering are rampant, these are only the symptoms of more basic difficulties which must be dealt with successfully along with any attempt to improve the standard of living. These difficulties have to do with human attitudes and the social and political structure. They are concerned not so much with a lack of technical knowledge (such as modern farming methods) although this kind of knowledge is important, but with a lack of social competence and of a social and political organization through which that competence can be developed and expressed.

In the newly developing countries countless millions of

people, the majority of whom live in peasant villages, lack the incentive to apply themselves to the task of improvement. People everywhere want better conditions and a richer economy, but after centuries of mental and physical starvation, the people have no confidence in themselves or in the idea that there is anything they can do to change the situation. The great masses are not only unaware of how to go about helping themselves, they frequently are not aware of the fact that self-help is a possibility. Ancient customs, a fatalistic outlook on life, long established attitudes of resignation and superstition, a deeply ingrained set of fears and suspicions, and rigid social and cultural patterns act as powerful blocks against the people's initiating any effective action of their own toward social or economic progress. Millions feel strongly that things are not as they ought to be, but they do not know why, and they do not know what steps they can take except to revolt.

Thus, the communities in these countries do not provide an environment that stimulates the people to seek self-improvement by constructive efforts, to receive and make use of the knowledge offered by technicians, or to search out ways and means of solving problems. When a technician comes in to teach them something from his specialized field the people are apt to either reject what he has to say, listen passively, or, perhaps after long and diligent efforts at education and persuasion by the technician, they may reluctantly try out one or two of his ideas. The peasant villages of the world are, in short, extremely resistant toward the recommendations that commonly come from standard American technical specialties. And it is highly doubtful that this resistance can be sufficiently worn down by traditional United States technical assistance to make possible a major change in the standard of living in these countries in anything less than several generations, if it can be accomplished at all by that means.

Meanwhile, the fact is that in the face of relentless Communist efforts to take over more and more countries and to rule the world, American foreign aid does not have several generations in which to help bring about a major change in the standard of living in Latin America, Africa, the Middle East, and Asia. It does not have one generation. It may have only a few years, and in some countries no more than a few months. And it does not have enough money.

But this is only one aspect of the difficulty.

From a long tradition of authoritarian control and exploitation at the hands of a highly centralized government and members of the elite, the people not only have no confidence in their own ability, they also have no confidence that their own government is really interested in them except for purposes of exploitation. Over the years a feeling of distrust toward government has become so firmly established in the public mind as to effectively separate the government from the people, thus making for continued turmoil and instability. To add to this difficulty, the national government in most of these countries is not able to reverse this public opinion by communicating any concern it might now have for the people, or by finding out what they really want so that it can respond to their wishes, because it has no effective way of projecting itself into the villages where most of the people live or of making itself felt in a favorable way in their daily activities.

There is in the vast majority of these countries no institution of local government, and even in those countries where efforts are now being made in this direction effective local government is only beginning to emerge. Likewise, other democratic institutions such as informal or voluntary organizations that would contribute to the development of local autonomy and provide a practical vehicle for self-expression, civic initiative, and the emergence of democratic leadership are either non-existent or poorly developed. Thus, the concept of making decisions to help themselves, engaging in planning, and taking action to make needed improvements by their own labors is yet to be established in the thinking of most of the people.

As a consequence of these social deficiencies the great mass of people in the less developed areas of the world have never known what it means to think for themselves or to exercise self-determination in ordering their lives. For generations there have been no institutions through which this was possible; there has been no motivation for the majority of the people to be anything other than subservient to whatever the ruling classes have imposed upon them. In the absence of local institutions, and with no adequate national machinery for bridging the gulf that separates the people from their governments, it has been impossible to build anything approaching a truly concerted effort between government and people.

Thus, millions are now ripe for agitation and violence because no satisfactory peaceful alternative has yet been established for bringing the government and people together in a mutual effort for the common good. In the sweep of social revolution now spreading over the world the ancient patterns of subservience and resignation are beginning to break; political distrust and powerful undercurrents of unrest are enabling the agents of international communism increasingly to cut away even the little remaining time that democracy has to prove its capacity for meeting the needs of man.

Under these conditions it should be obvious that no amount of economic aid or technical assistance rendered in accordance with the standard operating procedures of American specialization will be sufficient to deal with the basic difficulties of the underdeveloped world, or to serve adequately the national interest of the United States. If democracy is to meet the present world revolutionary challenge it is imperative that viable institutions be established in the newly emerging countries, at both community and national levels, through which the growing restlessness of the masses may be channeled constructively toward nation-building ends by democratic means. If this is not done, and done quickly, it is doubtful that most of the world will be able to survive as a free society. It is this task that makes community development an essential instrument to successful foreign aid.

If properly understood and carried out on a nationwide scale community development may be viewed as a powerful political instrument which will enable government to project its services into the thousands of local communities where people live, in such a way as to create within the minds of the people a sense of confidence in government. It may at the same time infuse into the agencies of government a heightened sense of public service, and it may bring about a degree of coordination among these agencies that will add to the efficient utilization of resources, both foreign and domestic. By creating and firmly establishing within the social fabric a sense of mutual trust between government and people, a national program of community development will make it possible to mobilize on a voluntary basis the collective energies of the people themselves in partnership with those of the government and to thus mount a vast, nationwide, unified effort directed toward the building of a stable and progressive state—while at the same time raising the social and economic standards of community and national life.

A national program of community development properly carried out will have the immediate effect of reducing the level of political distrust and social unrest; of creating a national atmosphere of peace and order; and thereby reducing the effects of further Communist infiltration. Thus, additional time may be provided in which to demonstrate the capacity of democracy to bring about the long-range social and economic changes that must be made if the conditions of human misery and deprivation that now exist throughout the less developed areas of the world are to be eliminated.

In view of the urgency of community development to the peace of the world, it is unfortunate that the term by which this concept has come to be known has been interpreted in so many different ways. This failure in definition and in practice has resulted in a worldwide failure to understand properly a basic concept for which this term is only a symbol. Many people in many countries use the same term but proceed on the basis of widely different ideas as to what it means.

Probably the most common error, and perhaps the most unfortunate, repeated in country after country, has been the false assumption that the end purpose of community development is material improvements. So much emphasis has been placed on physical and economic improvements as ends in themselves that many people have lost sight of the fact that the prime purpose of community development is to build and strengthen the processes of a free, self-determining society in order to provide man with an environment which in itself creates initiative for the responsible solution of problems. Physical improvements are an inevitable and essential part of community development. However, these improvements are not to be regarded as ends in themselves, but simply as instruments of stimulation that are used as a part of the broad process of helping people to establish for themselves a participating, problem-solving society in which the chief concern is the dignity and well-being of individuals. And unless physical improvements are accomplished in this way they make little contribution toward the development of that kind of a society.

At the local level, a program of community development is designed to deal with the community as a whole, and is focused upon the over-all well-being of that total unit. From this perspective all functions and activities that go into the community's total makeup are taken into consideration in terms of their interrelationships to each other and to the whole. Community development in the emergent countries is internal development by the people themselves in active partnership with their national government on all fronts and in every aspect of the community's total life. Once this broad process is organized and set in motion each specific improvement will contribute to strengthening the total process, resulting in turn in more changes and improvements, again heightening the total process, releasing still more human energy, resulting in still more changes and improvements. It is therefore of the utmost importance that no one specific improvement be handled as an isolated project unrelated to the whole, but that all specific improvements be accomplished as integral parts of the total over-all operation.

One of the primary aims of such a program is the cultivation of democratic institutions both in the form of voluntary civic associations and in the form of local government, nurturing initiative and self-determination. A properly implemented community development operation will cause the people to see their situation in a new light, realize new hope for its improvement, and experience the satisfaction of growth in their capacity for achievement. They will acquire increasing ability to recognize opportunities, understand and cope intelligently with limitations, and organize themselves effectively for collective study, planning, and action. Community development programs comprehensively and systematically aim at fostering individual and group traits such as a sense of social and political responsibility, a growth in civic consciousness, leadership, alertness, sensitivity, creative thought, idealism, and concern for human needs. Such progressive attitudes will enable people to differ with each other without destroying their basic unity.

From the national viewpoint, community development is a program in which the great mass of the population, community by community, moves increasingly toward greater independence and self-reliance, while at the same time developing a broadening awareness of the interrelationships and responsibilities which must be assumed among all communities and regions within a country for the building of nationhood. In this process each community in the nation will become increasingly receptive to, and more able to make use of, outside technical and material aid.

Such a new willingness to accept change, for instance, will substantially reduce the difficulty of getting peasant farmers to adopt better methods of agriculture, reducing the hunger problem at the same time. The same principle will apply equally to small business development, public health and sanitation, education, housing, homemaking, recreation, transportation, and to all other facets of community life.

Community development from the national point of view is a nationwide process creating within all communities of the nation qualities of effective local organization, cooperation, enterprise, and capacity for change, and joining these qualities with the nation-building efforts of the government as a whole.

In many countries around the world heroic struggles are being made by dedicated and little-known persons to establish or carry on programs of community development. Actually, there are relatively few programs in the world that really qualify as community development as I have defined it in this account. But from the many efforts that have been made, it is clear that there are certain minimum requirements that must be accepted if the goals of community development are to be realized.

The first of these requirements is that the program must be launched and carried out on a nationwide scale. This does not mean that excellent results are not being accomplished by many local programs; but unless operations are established on a nationwide scale, the essential linkage between government and people cannot be achieved. This means that the national government must assume the leading role, with all major private and religious interests working in cooperation with the government and lending their active leadership and support. The program must have the personal and aggressive leadership of the nation's chief executive, such as President Magsaysay supplied in the Philippines.

The government must make community development a major aim of national policy and give official recognition to its importance. The program should have a central place in the national budget to ensure necessary financial, material, and technical support based upon the expressed needs of the people as they come to light during the program. As matters now stand in most of the emergent nations too large a proportion of the national budget is being devoted to development projects that are determined by politicians and bureaucrats at the top, usually with the advice of foreign aid officials, in which the people have no say, with which the people can establish no personal identification, and which therefore make little, if any, contribution to a viable political and social order able to resist the continued danger of political unrest, violent revolt, and Communist takeover.

A two-way channel of communications is imperative between all levels of government and the residents of the local communities so that the government can learn the people's wishes, and so that the people can learn the problems of the government. This will make it possible to give the people an actual voice in national decision-making and demonstrate the sincerity of the government's interest in them. As soon as the government is prepared to make good on its community development policy, that policy should be communicated throughout the nation by every means available.

A national community development agency, such as that in the Philippines, should be created to provide full-time professional community development service at all levels of national life, and this agency should be attached to the top level of government. This agency should have legal authority to deal with international aid organizations, and it should be able to work cooperatively with representatives of authority from all appropriate agencies in the country, either inside or outside the government, for policy and planning purposes. Responsibility for the agency's management and operations should reside in a top administrator responsible directly to the chief executive of the nation, not to a board or committee, or to one of the ministers.

The detailed organizational arrangement best suited to any given country must be designed individually. But whatever the organizational pattern may be, certain responsibilities should be clearly assigned to the national community development agency. These responsibilities should include the scheduling of geographical areas in which operations of varying intensity are to be conducted as the program spreads over the country, the setting of priorities for starting these operations, and the determination of the work to be performed depending upon local needs and budgetary and personnel limitations.

The community development agency should coordinate the services supplied to the effort by other agencies, and it should have the responsibility of employing, training, and supervising a full-time corps of professional community development workers. It should also be responsible for organizing and conducting special training sessions for officials and employees in all branches of government whose services will be needed in the operations, and for other persons outside the government whose understanding and support will be essential. These training sessions and conferences, along with other media of communication, should be directed toward gaining and continuously increasing public acceptance of the program.

The national agency should also be responsible for establishing a research and evaluation unit attached directly to the agency, or arranged through contracts with appropriate institutions such as universities and private consulting firms. In the interest of objectivity, the research and evaluation should be conducted separately from the regular service functions of the operating field staff, and should provide sufficient information for use in long-range planning as well as for the immediate purpose of improving the management, operational, and training aspects of the program.

It is impossible to over-emphasize the importance of the full-time professional community development workers which the national agency should provide. Without them the potential of a national community development program cannot be realized. It must be recognized that the art of community development is in itself an occupational skill requiring a full-time practitioner especially trained for that purpose. It is not merely a job for the garden variety of so-called multi-purpose or village-level workers that have been so widely discussed all over the world, nor is it something that can be done as a sideline or as an extra chore tacked onto the duties of other types of personnel. An effective arrangement could be made in which the typical multi-purpose or village-level workers could be used as aides to community development workers, but inasmuch as the job of a true community development worker is one of the most difficult of all tasks, requiring a high level of personal skill and ability, and is one of the most vital in the whole process of nation-building, it is a job that must be filled by a higher grade of personnel than has been commonly thought necessary in most of the emergent countries where community development programs have been attempted.

It is primarily because of a failure to recognize these facts that so many programs operating in various parts of the world under the name of community development have fallen short of their goals, and in practice have not actually been community development. This has been unfortunate. It has added to the worldwide confusion over the meaning of the term. It has damaged the reputation of the movement. And it has had the effect of masking the potential that true community development offers for the purpose of breathing democratic life and vitality into the national society.

The community development worker must be able to visualize as a unit all of the physical and social factors that together comprise the community, and must thoroughly comprehend the broad concept of community development. Unless he clearly understands this concept, continuously points his work toward the goals it embraces, and avoids confusing the means with the ends, he cannot be effective.

He should have a persuasive and dynamic personality, but also possess the qualities of warmth, humility, and infinite patience. He must be thoroughly dedicated to his mission and skilled in the arts of organization and leadership; he must have deep personal respect for the people with whom he works. He must be adept at leading and instilling enthusiasm in large community gatherings, at leading small group discussions, at counseling with individuals, at moving from study to planning to action, and he must be able to develop these same skills in the people. He must be able to function as a personal confidant, a teacher, a leader, a stimulator, a guide, an ally, a friend. He must be able to lift the people's spirits, inspire confidence, help them to grow creatively, and make greater and more effective use of their powers for constructive achievement. The community development worker will establish a close personal rapport with the community, and thereby begin the essential working relationship and two-way channel of communication that must exist between the people and the government.

All relevant government agencies must be included in the program. This is necessary because sufficient technical personnel must be made available from each of the various fields of specialization that will be needed in the operations which the community development workers will set in motion in local communities throughout the nation. This will include such important fields as agriculture, industrial development, home economics, public health and sanitation, education, public works, housing, recreation, and others that are related to specific improvements in the various facets and activities of community life. These specialized services should be brought together in an integrated pattern of operation and introduced to the local communities by the community development workers within the framework of the ongoing program of the local citizens' organization.

This means that as the workers proceed with their job of helping the people to organize, study, plan, and act for the comprehensive development of their communities, technical personnel from the various fields of specialization will be brought into the communities at strategic times that the worker must be able to judge. If carried out as an integral part of the total community development program, each specific action project can be used as a means of stimulating and strengthening the total program, thus accomplishing results far greater than that specific project. The supporting specialists should not be employed by the national community development agency, but should be fed into the effort on a coordinated basis by their respective agencies.

A further requirement is that provision be made for providing the communities with adequate assistance in the form of tools, equipment, materials, and supplies to ensure the successful completion of important local projects. The criteria for determining when and to what extent this type of aid is to be made available should be a willingness of the people to invest their own energies and resources in a given project up to the limits of their ability, the feasibility of the project from the standpoint of sound development practice, and financial limitations.

Care must be taken in the handling of this aid to avoid creating an undue dependence upon the government. However, if properly managed this kind of aid can become a valuable instrument for helping the communities to gain a sense of achievement by enabling them to complete important improvements that would not otherwise be possible. Under skillful handling this will have the effect of strengthening the basic democratic process that is being evolved by the community development program, thereby spurring the community to still greater initiative and self-determination. It will produce dramatic results in terms of building nationwide confidence in government, and it can also become a valuable technique for helping people to become increasingly adept at understanding and adjusting to practical limitations. It is the art of guiding the people to this kind of understanding and ability to make intelligent adjustments, while at the same time developing a maximum state of readiness for the effective use of outside aid along with local resources, that constitutes one of the major responsibilities of the community development worker.

The formation of suitable administrative machinery is prerequisite to successful community development operations on a nationwide scale, but of all the possible operations of government, this is probably the one operation that can be most easily killed by excessive bureaucracy. For in the final analysis this type of development is deeply personal, and if it is to thrive it must be kept that way. For example, India's greatest community development worker was Mahatma Gandhi, who went into the villages and infused into the people a quality of greatness they had not known before he came. Without that element of personality, or spirit, or soul, or feeling, or what Elisa Molina de Stahl in Guatemala calls "social emotion," true community development will not take place.

In this age of emphasis on efficiency, specialization, business-like procedures, and material values it is not easy to preserve the elements of "social emotion" and the personal touch in a government agency. Yet that is precisely what must be done in the national community development agency if it is to succeed in its mission. And it is for this reason that finding a person who possesses that faculty to head the agency is another major requirement for an effective national program.

Without a Ramon P. Binamira, the executive action of President Magsaysay could not have been implemented with the personal drive and the mixture of idealism and shrewdness that has made the operations of the PACD one of the outstanding demonstrations of community development in the world. Elisa Molina de Stahl is another example of the kind of leadership that a national program of community development requires. This, then, is one of the important clues to what must be done to promote such a program. Someone must take action to ferret out and support these leaders.

But these leaders can only be found if the person doing the searching knows what he is looking for. The leader to look for should not only have a thorough comprehension of the community development idea, but should be one who is willing to fight for it with militant vigor and who knows how to fight effectively. Ideally, because of the nature of things in the emergent countries, he should belong to the elite class of the society and have wealth and power of his own or have ready access to that kind of influence for use when needed. He should have the fibre to resist the pressures of partisan politics that will inevitably be brought against the program, he should be an organizer and administrator, he should have the ability to inspire, and the capacity for compassion.

These are some of the requirements for successful national community development programs in the newly developing countries of the world. And what does it mean to America? It means simply this: Community development is a powerful force which American government aid and American private aid may support and promote to help millions of people translate their democratic ideals into democratic action to build a world environment for peace and human happiness. This is how America may rise to the ideals of her own revolution and meet the new revolutionary challenge of the twentieth century.

READINGS

Books

ABUEVA, JOSE V. *Focus on the Barrio.* Manila: Institute of Public Administration, University of the Philippines, 1959.

ALLEN, HAROLD B. *Rural Reconstruction in Action: Experience in the Near East.* Ithaca, New York: Cornell University Press, 1953.

BATTEN, T. R. *Communities and Their Development.* London: Oxford University Press, 1957.

DAYAL, RAJESHWAR. *Community Development Programme in India.* Bombay: Kitab Mahal Publishers, 1960.

DUBE, S. C. *Indian Village.* London: Routledge & Kegan Paul Ltd., 1959.

FLUHARTY, VERNON LEE. *Dance of the Millions: Military Rule and Social Revolution in Colombia.* Pittsburgh: University of Pittsburgh Press, 1957.

A Guide to Community Development. Issued by Government of India. New Delhi: Coronation Printing Works, 1957.

MAYER, ALBERT, *et al. Pilot Project India: The Story of Rural Development at Etawah, Uttar Pradesh.* Berkeley: University of California Press, 1958.

MORAES, FRANK. *India Today.* New York: The Macmillan Co., 1960.

NELSON, HENRY B. (ed.). *Community Education: Principles and Practices from World-Wide Experiences.* Chicago: University of Chicago Press, 1959.

Regional Development for Regional Peace: A New Policy and Program to Counter the Soviet Menace in the Middle East. Washington, D. C.: The Public Affairs Institute, undated.

Technical Assistance: Final Report of the Committee on Foreign

Relations. Congressional Report No. 139, Washington, D. C.: Government Printing Office, 1957.

United States Government Organization Manual, 1960-1961. Washington, D. C.: Government Printing Office, 1960.

Articles and Other Documents

CARE in Colombia. A report. New York: Cooperative for American Relief Everywhere, Inc., 1959.

CARE in India. A report. New York: Cooperative for American Relief Everywhere, Inc., 1960.

CARE in Vietnam. A report. New York: Cooperative for American Relief Everywhere, Inc., 1959.

CARE Philippines Program, The. New York: Cooperative for American Relief Everywhere, Inc., 1960.

Colombia Community Development: A Survey Report. New York: Cooperative for American Relief Everywhere, Inc., 1960.

Community Development: A handbook prepared by a study conference on community development held at Hartwell House, Aylesbury, Buckinghamshire, September, 1957. London: Her Majesty's Stationery Office, 1958.

Community Development and Its Role in Nation Building. Report of the Inter-Regional Conference on Community Development and its Role in Nation Building, Seoul, Korea, May 6-12, 1961.

Community Development: Concept and Description. A background paper for the 1961 Inter-Regional Community Development Conference, Seoul, Korea, May 6-12, 1961.

Community Development and Related Services. New York: United Nations Publication, 1960.

Community Development Research Council's Annual Report. Manila: University of the Philippines, 1959.

Community Development Review. Issues from 1956-1961, Washington, D. C.: International Cooperation Administration.

DE CLERCK, M. *Notes on Education for Social Changes.* United Nations Educational, Scientific, and Cultural Organization (UNESCO), Paris, 1960.

DOOLEY, DELMER J. *The Near East Foundation Program of Rural Development in the Varamin Plains of Iran, 1946-1959.* New York: Near East Foundation, 1959.

EINSIEDEL, LUZ. *Success and Failure in Community Development in Batangas.* Community Development Research Council. Manila: University of the Philippines, undated.

ENSMINGER, DOUGLAS. *The Ford Foundation Program Letter: India.* Report No. 108. New York: May 1, 1959.

Executive Order No. 156. President of Philippines, Manila, 1956.

FIRMALINO, TITO C. *Political Activities of Barrio Citizens in Iloilo as They Affect Community Development.* Community Development Research Council. Manila: University of the Philippines, undated.

Ford Foundation and Foundation Supported Activities in India, The. New York: January 1, 1960.

KAPLAN, GABRIEL, AND SAMPER, RAFAEL, M. D. *A Plan to Integrate Colombia's Private and Public Sectors in Its Community Development Program for Socio-Economic Improvement of Its Veredas and Barrios.* Bogotá: 1961.

KRISHNAMACHARI, V. T. Community Development in India. New Delhi: Government of India Publication, 1958.

"Latin America's Nationalistic Revolutions," *The Annals of the American Academy of Political and Social Science.* New York: March, 1961.

LEAGANS, J. PAUL. *Elements of Extension Education Process Related to Community Development.* New Delhi: January, 1960.

LUTZ, EDWARD A. *The Role of Local Government in Philippine Democracy.* Manila: University of the Philippines, College of Agriculture, July, 1958.

MARIS, PAUL V. *Report Proposing Point IV Project for Aiding Purchasers of Crown Lands in Iran,* May 28, 1952.

Personnel for the Mutual Security Program. Washington, D. C.: Government Printing Office, 1957.

Political Implications of Community Development. A background paper for the 1961 Inter-Regional Community Development Conference, Seoul, Korea, May 6-12, 1961.

POLSON, ROBERT A. *A Report on the Training Aspects of the Philippine Community Development Program.* Manila: International Cooperation Administration, 1960.

PONGIS, PETER. A series of unpublished addresses, Royal National Foundation, Athens, Greece.

Presidential Assistant on Community Development, The. Annual report, Manila, 1958.

PACD Evaluation Survey Bulletin, The. Manila: Presidential Assistant on Community Development, 1959.

A Report of Agricultural Extension Work in the United States of America and Reorganization of Extension Services in Pakistan. Karachi: Government of Pakistan Press, 1951.

Reports and Publications on local government in Philippines. Presidential Assistant on Community Development, Manila.

Reports and Publications. International Cooperation Administration, Washington, D. C.

Reports and Publications. Presidential Assistant on Community Development, Republic of Philippines, Manila.

Reports and Publications relative to community development. Government of India, New Delhi.

Reports and Publications relative to community development. Government of Iran, Tehran.

Reports and Publications relative to community development. Government of Pakistan, Karachi.

Reports and Publications relative to community development. Republic of Guatemala, Guatemala City.

Reports and Publications relative to community development. Republic of Korea, Seoul.

Reports and Publications relative to community development. Republic of Vietnam, Saigon.

Reports and Publications relative to community development. Royal National Foundation, Athens, Greece.

Review of the Second Seven-Year Plan Program of Iran. Division of Economic Affairs, Tehran, Iran, March 10, 1960.

SINGH, TARLOK. The Cooperative Village. New Delhi: Government of India, 1958.

Social Progress through Community Development. New York: United Nations Publication, 1955.

Study of the Grants-in-Aid Projects of the Presidential Assistant on Community Development, A. Community Development Research Council, Manila: University of the Philippines, 1959.

Study Kit on Training for Community Development. United Nations Publication, New York, December, 1957.

Syllabus for Orientation Training of Community Development Personnel. Ministry of Community Development, Government of India Press, Faridabad, 1958.

TAYLOR, CARL C. *A Critical Analysis of India's Community Development Programme.* Issued by the Community Project Administration, Government of India, New Delhi, 1956.

United Nations Series on Community Development—Community Leadership. United Nations Publication, New York, February, 1960.

Village Aid. Karachi: Government of Pakistan Press, 1956.

VILLANUEVA, BUENAVENTURA M. *The Barrio People.* Community Development Research Council, Manila: University of the Philippines, 1959.

VILLANUEVA, PATROCINIO S. *The Value of Rural Roads.* Community Development Research Council, Manila: University of the Philippines, 1959.

What Municipal Mayors Say About Local Autonomy and Community Development. A report on the Seminar for Municipal Mayors of the Philippines on Local Autonomy and Community Development, held at the Community Development Center, Laguna, April 3-5, 1959.

INDEX

Act for International Development
(1961), 66-67
Agency for International Development (US), 180
Agriculture:
improvement in Greek, 156-157
in India, 76
in Point Four Program, 54-59, 61
Alderfer, E. Gordon, 174
Alliance for Progress, 27, 30
American Friends Service Committee, 172
Arbenz, Jacobo, 6, 10, 15
Arévalo, Juan José, 4, 6
Armas, Castillo, 13-17, 19
Attitudes:
in emergent countries toward community development, 180-182
United States, on community development, 176-180

Barrett, Al, 18, 21
Barrio Charter Act (Philippines),
109
Bernhart, Richard V., 124
Berry, L. A., 19
Binamira, Ramon P., 97-106, 108-111,
113-114, 117-124, 193
Blind, Guatemalan program for, 6-14
Bogotá Conference of Foreign Ministers, 35
Bowles, Chester, 89
Bureaucracy:
community development programs
and, 54-59, 61-67, 178
ICA and, 50-52
Indian community development program and, 79-86
Philippine community development
program and, 96, 118-126

Camargo, Alberto Lleras, 41-42
Catherwood Foundation (Bryn
Mawr), 94
CARE:
community development program
in Colombia and, 42-43, 45
Greek community development program and, 152, 155-163
importance of, in community development, 174-175
in Iran, 146
in Mexico, 170-173
in Philippines, 95
self-help programs of, 163-175
in South Korea, 169
South Vietnam program of, 163-169
Caste system, in India, 74
Castro, Fidel, 35, 37
CDPC. *See* Community Development
Planning Council (Philippines)
Chadwick, Edward R., 124
Colombia, community development
program in, 41-45
Committee for Philippine Action in
Development, Reconstruction, and
Education, 94
Communism:
community development and, 181-
182
in Greece, 153-154
in Guatemala, 4, 5, 10-12, 13-14
in Iran, 133-134, 135, 145
in Latin America, 27, 30, 32, 40, 45
in South Vietnam, 167-168
Community centers:
in Greece, 157-158, 161-162
in Philippines, 97
Community development:
attitudes in emergent countries and,
180-182
bureaucracy and, 54-59, 61-67, 178